Now I Can Sit
With the Old Men

Journeys on the Road to Wisdom

Margaret L. Bishop

First published in the United States in 2009 by Margaret L. Bishop

Cover design by Kevin R. Sartin

ISBN 978-0-578-02582-7

Not all who wander are lost.

J. R. R. Tolkien

All I have asked of my travels is that they test me and they teach me and in that I have succeeded. I have written this book for Jakub, Katherine, Duncan, Will, Celia, Yacob, and Ben, that they may be inspired to travel the world and learn, as I have.

My stories, every one of them true, are dedicated to those very extraordinary friends and family who have helped make them come true. They are dedicated to….

- *Annabel,* whose courage and compassion were a beacon of light;
- *Awa* and *Adama,* who taught me more than my words can explain;
- *Daidie,* who sat with his rifle so I could sleep on his roof;
- *Dave,* whose empathy helped me heal from the haunting sounds of mortar attacks;
- *Greg,* who gave up his vacation to see me to health;
- *Richard,* who laughs at my stories, brags to his friends, and tells me he's proud;
- *Rick,* who shared broad shoulders to cry on and an attentive ear;
- *Sunshine,* in his Civil Affairs uniform, who always lit up the room with that broad smile he so readily flashed;
- *Mis amigos cariñosos,* who protected me, made me blush, and made me laugh;
- *My courageous and courteous PSD* who risked their own lives for mine;
- *My father,* who instilled in me the importance of travel and who reassured me that going somewhere *just because I want to* is a perfectly acceptable excuse;
- *All the individuals* who made my stories a reality and who made my voyages unique;
    and
- *My guardian angel* who has more than once worked overtime.

A friend once told me
she wants the bed next to mine in the old folks' home.

*I would be telling strange stories
and everyone would think I had gone mad,* she said,
but she would know the tales I was telling are true.

Only a few names that follow are changed.

Contents

❧

Prologue

I was born to travel. It is in my ancestry. It is in my genes. It is the way I was raised. My father's family spread its wings and flew to the distant corners of ancient civilizations and far-flung cultures, well before many Americans did. My mother's forbears helped forge America's *Oregon Trail*. My parents sent me on my first plane ride before my first birthday; they sent me overseas alone when I was just fifteen. They told me there were places to explore, people to meet, lessons to learn. The world became my school.

In the years since, I have continued to travel far and wide, for both personal pleasure and work. Today my economic development consulting takes me to far continents, foreign countries, big cities, and remote villages all over the globe. It gives me privileged invitations into businesses, government offices, ceremonies, meetings, and private homes. Without those experiences I would have a much less rich and a much less realistic view of the world, and a much less informed understanding of myself. My work and the people it has given me the honor to meet, have crafted the lens through which I see the world and myself today.

This book recounts some of the adventures I have had and a few of the lessons I have learned.

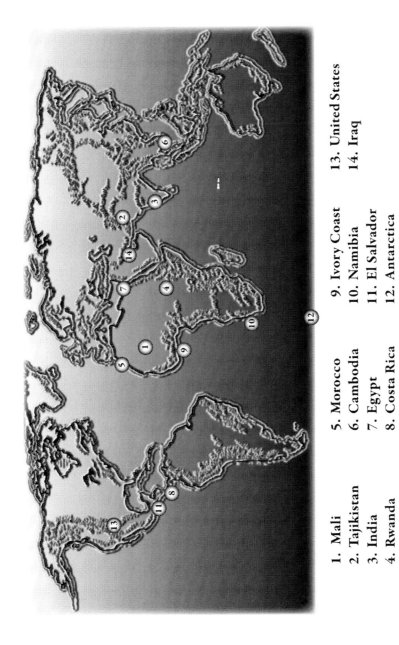

1. Mali
2. Tajikistan
3. India
4. Rwanda

5. Morocco
6. Cambodia
7. Egypt
8. Costa Rica

9. Ivory Coast
10. Namibia
11. El Salvador
12. Antarctica

13. United States
14. Iraq

School Starts

Mali (1991 – 1994)

If you set foot in one hundred lands
you can sit with the old men.

Malian saying

The sun rose early that late January dawn, bringing with it a realization that I was in fact *there*. A strange land which only days before had been a faraway dream. It beckoned me with outstretched hands, its real reach yet unknown. It called me with bright sunshine, a broad smile, a firm grip, and sad eyes. After smug weeks of telling friends I was off to an adventure, one that would surely change my life, I had arrived. How naïve I had been. Yes, it would change my life; it would lead me down a new and uncharted path, but little did I know how or why. *A Kodak moment*, I had imagined. How quaint. That was before reality hit like a ton of bricks. That was before the throes of dysentery that would wrench my gut and the malaria fevers that would color my nights. That was before the mosquitoes, the heat, the rain, the dust, and the dirt.

For better and for worse, I was there.

As the daylight emerged, a rooster crowed. Like someone rustling plastic wrap in a quiet room, it broke the silence with an annoying sound I could not ignore. How strange it seems to me today, years later, after time has passed and oceans were crossed, that of all the sights and sounds, the call of a rooster still transports me back to that first morning in Africa, the moment reality dawned with the sun.

I had committed myself for two years to a life and a people I did not know, for reasons I do not yet understand. The rooster crowed and my surroundings began to take tangible, substantive shape. The skip of my heart and new quickness of my breath bore witness to that unspoken fear of an unknown that I had only recently embraced, so easy it had seemed in the familiar comfort of a sunny apartment an ocean away. But now I was really there. The plane had landed in the early hours of the day. Pots of kerosene sat burning on the runway to light the way. A roar of cheers and clapping arose as the wheels touched down. A safe landing. *Praise be to Allah*, a chorus of voices called out. The bus I boarded for the ride into town roared through what was left of the night, piercing the darkness and fog. Brush fires burned low, their yellow and orange glow pressed flat against the black of night as we sped forth to the little village of *Katibougou*, the place that was to become my new home.

In the chill of that first early morning I came to consciousness slowly as if awakening from a deep, long dream. A shiver raced firmly up my back, one half centimeter at a time. Again a rooster crowed. I was there. I was really there. Africa. *The Dark Continent*, it is sometimes called. Why *dark*? Because of a fear of the unknown? A prejudice that unfortunately still runs deep? The color of people's skin? The depth of the jungle, the sound of a lion's roar, or the intensity of a gorilla's stare? What about the brightness and light of a strong sun? The cleansing of a heavy monsoon rain? The white of a mosque or the sparkle in a child's eye? A woman's hope? A man's dream?

Through a lifting haze, the shapes became clear and strong. The gnarled reach of a *Baobab* tree. A klatch of round huts each with its own conical straw hat. The distant hills. The silhouette of a bird taking flight.

People gradually took form. Women pounded grain in an age-old rhythm of poverty and a life trapped in time. An awakening night guard slowly sat up. A mangy, bone-thin dog with one crippled leg skipped by.

What have I done? I asked myself as I followed my gray canvas duffel bag through the village dust; it rode high atop a woman's head. That bag I had struggled to drag through the airport, she carried with ease. *Fatumata* moved with dignity, without a thought of complaint. She carried with her a burden others readily handed off. She was to become my mother, my African mom. *Fatumata* was the one who taught me, though I was the older one of our pair. She was the one who would guide me through life. She shared her food, her family, her spirit, her home. This woman gave me my African name. She was the mother who laughed at the mistakes I made, not with malice but in good-hearted fun. *We were better entertainment than TV*, a missionary later said. My new adoptive mother was the one who scolded me when I came home covered in red clay dust; she ushered me to the bathing area outside, a bucket of warm, fire-heated water in hand. She washed my clothes, worried when I hitchhiked into town, and issued me warnings to take caution and exercise care.

With the strength and grounding of so many African women, *Fatumata* showed me the way, all the while carrying that gray duffel bag through the village to my new home. Soon I would sleep in a mud hut with a thatched roof, two metal beds, a tiny window, and a corrugated sheet metal door. With broad, flat, brown spiders on the walls and dust on the concrete floor, I learned to sweep my new palace of mud and cement and straw each day, but not at night. *That would disturb the spirits*, the villagers said. *Sweep your house when the morning is bright and the day is fresh*, they advised. Slowly I learned to live in a quiet truce with those spiders that in my childhood had engendered one of my greatest fears, that at a young age had made me cry, and as an adult still made me shudder and wince.

Africa. *I was really there.* It is a continent that conquers many, forgives some, motivates a few, and touches all. A land that in one day can just as easily bless or curse. A continent whose life gives rhythm to the soul of a woman and the hips of a man. Whose children warm the heart with a broad smile, a giggle, and a quick laugh. Africa. It is a continent that, in my experience, seethes with anger and teems with hope. It is a place that teaches pain because a life is at once cheap but dear. *I was really there.* Africa. *Mali.* What led me to believe that *I*, a spoiled white woman from the cornfields and apple trees of the American Midwest, was any match for what was to come?

As the days passed and the weeks stretched on, a routine emerged. I learned the language and a new way of life. I learned to bathe from a bucket, to wash my clothes by hand. I learned to buy my food daily for there was no refrigerator to keep it fresh in the sweltering West African heat.

From that village of six hundred I moved several hours south to a city filled with people and traffic and noise. Where the seasons changed, the dry earth cracked, and the temperatures soared before thick black clouds roared across a thunderous indigo sky as the monsoons of the rainy season approached. *Sikasso* was a city bright with the red-orange flowers of the *Flamboyant* tree bursting like a shower of silent firecrackers against the dark brown branches and the blue sky. But it was also a city loaded with the smell of open sewers hanging heavy in the air and the buzz of a thousand mosquitoes that serenaded me unfailingly each night. In a country largely covered by the *Sahara* Desert, this was the place where crops grew well. Where termite mounds tower six feet tall. Where my neighbor died painfully from the bite of a rabid dog. It was a place abundant in vegetables and fruit on a continent where many starve. This was the land where the hunters danced under the bright light of a full moon. There I passed two of the best and hardest years of my life.

Sikasso, a city of one hundred thousand, lies in a region known for its hunters; they are fiercely traditional men with unwavering animist beliefs. Revered for their courage, respected for their physical prowess, the hunters are feared for mysterious powers rooted deeply in another, less physical world. Dressed in garb the dull color of dry earth or the color of the rough bark of a sturdy tree, they venture far into the bush, *en brousse*, giving chase to the few wild animals that still wander this ragged, mud- and dust-covered terrain. A couple of monkeys, a variety of snakes, the odd rodent, maybe a small deer or a wild cat. Today only the very old men talk of the days when the big animals still roamed West Africa. Chased away as the trees were cut and the *Sahara* moved south, a few migrating elephants are about all that now remain.

Lively and spirited men, these hunters of the South lead a hard but winsome life; they have souls that sing with the wind and beat with the drums. Their eyes light with the crack of a gun. When on special occasions they bring out the hand-carved wooden drums, they dance late, very, very late, into the star- and moon-lit night. Like madmen, their eyes awaken with fire and their bones spring to life. The sounds of their shotguns crack through the air as they leap wildly to a strong and raucous beat.

With an old rifle in hand and courage in their hearts, the hunters of *Sikasso* trudge deep into the dry grass and brown dust of the southern Mali bush. Counting for safe passage on the spirits of their animist beliefs, these men don hand-collected talismans of varied sorts. Strips of dark leather, bits of ivory-colored bone, assorted amulets, broken mirrors, and odd-shaped bits of glass adorn their hand-woven, hand-dyed tunics and hats. Spitting Cobras stir ominously as these men walk through the brush. With extraordinary accuracy this deadly snake propels its poison straight at its victim's eye. Only when confused by the reflected light of the scattered bits of shiny glass, does the cobra's venomous aim go fortuitously off its mark.

Though I had settled easily in *Sikasso*, three hundred-seventy kilometers to the south, that first Malian village of *Katibougou* had become my spiritual home. For years to come, *Katibougou* would provide me with a compass by which to navigate West African culture and life.

"*Hawa!*" she cried with joy in her voice and bright sparkles in her young eyes.

"*Hawa! Ne togoman*, my namesake," she said with remarkable pride as she took my hand, stood tall, and held her head up high, marching me over a well-worn, hardened dirt path. Just six years old, she had the responsibility and sense of someone five times her age. When we finally sat on stools in the family compound, my Malian sister and me, *Hawa* wrapped her arms around my waist and leaned in close with the innocence and affection that only a child has.

"Mama! Mama! *Hawa's* back!" she called out with unmistakable glee when her mother appeared.

"*Hawa*, welcome home. How are you? How's your health?" asked *Fatumata*, my mother, my teacher, my friend.

"Come see the new little one. *Moussokoro* gave birth last month."

Moussokoro was my unmarried fourteen-year old sister, a free spirit of sorts who loved life, flirted with the men, and danced in the night.

"*Hawa!*" called three-year old *Lassiné* as he, my little African brother, ran to me with his bare feet, dirty hands, and purulent, runny nose. After an absence of many months, I was back in the village, back in *Katibougou*. I was back in the loving embrace of my adoptive family. It felt good to be home.

As the night descended we sat outside on low, wooden stools and talked. The villagers wanted stories of the South, the fabled land my family and their neighbors had heard of but had never seen. It was the place of milk and honey where life was easy and food was plentiful and good. *Was I doing OK? Did I have a safe house? Were my neighbors kind to me, and good?* For hours we listened to the traditional music of a talented old man on his beloved *balafon*, the light sound of hand-twisted strings over hollowed-out gourds and split bamboo floating gently through the night like the scent of jasmine in the air. Someone else brought a drum, carefully crafted by skilled hands from the solid trunk of an old tree. The two little girls, *Hawa* and her seven-year old cousin *Bintou*, started to dance. Their slender bodies pulsed and flowed, moving with passion in the light of the silver-white moon. They danced, they shimmied, and they swayed uninhibited, to the warm beat of the music, sending electricity through the air as bright diamonds glistened against the black velvet night sky. It was a magical time that left a beautiful image well-etched in my mind.

To travel is to learn and during those years I learned what no classroom or school book can teach. I learned about love in Mali. The love of a child who gives openly and expects nothing in return, but who with the slightest of attention blossoms like a flower after the warm spring rain. I learned about love as I saw the look of a poor mother who guardedly held tight a newborn against great odds that this baby, too, would not live. Far too common is child death in Mali, robbing parents of one more precious mouth to feed. Strange to those of us from the West, you do not praise a newborn, but rather tell the mother what a puny little child it is, what a skinny little runt. Otherwise the spirits get jealous and claim yet another young life as their own. I learned, too, about love when I saw the heartbreaking plight of a mother forced to choose, with a tired body and a heavy heart, which newborn twin could live, knowing her breasts could not support both.

I learned about love when I feared little four-year old *Adama* would die. My landlady's grandson, he was wracked with the fever and dehydration of malaria. Normally bubbly, a chatter-box with a captivating smile, round cheeks, always a fresh giggle on his lips and bright sunshine in his eyes, he was listless, his eyes dull, his skin loose and dry; his normally animated body was as limp and gray as an old, wet rag.

Adama was the little one my neighbors called my shadow for after my early months he followed my footsteps everywhere I went. First fearful of me, getting terror in his eyes at my very sight, *Adama's* trepidation at my presence gradually gave way to a devotion I had not experienced before as over the months he learned my ways and I gained his trust. *He had been sick for two days*, my landlady said when I returned home to find him so gravely ill. He would no longer take food or water, she told me. Beside herself with worry, *Korotum* had decided, at more than sixty years old, to wrap young *Adama* on her own back for the long walk to the regional hospital, knowing the dirty, barren conditions there gave very little hope.

I took *Adama* in my arms, his frail bones covered with a dull sheet of sagging, dry skin. He fell into my embrace like a lumpy sack of potatoes, his head heavy, his arms and legs falling limp. His eyes barely opened as I held a small spoon of juice to his dry, chalky lips, but slowly he took a sip. It was the lifeline he drank for me but had refused from everyone else.

"He would not drink for me anymore," *Korotum* said, with the tired eyes, resignation, and despair of an old woman who has seen life come and has seen it go.

A few sips of juice were all he would take, even from me. He would drink no more. I cradled him in my arms as *Korotum* and I set off, walking three and a half miles under the burning mid-morning sun. If ever there were a color divide, it disappeared as we quickly became one family, as I became the mother, and little *Adama* became my son. If only for moments the jealous spirits looked down and saw that on that one day they not only tangled with *Adama*; they also reckoned with me.

An injection of imported *Nivaquine* saved young *Adama* that day.

"*Hawa!*" he chirped, days later and once again full of sparkle and spunk.

"What are we having for dinner?" he called through my screen door.

Only moments before I had heard *Korotum* call him for dinner.

"*Oh no*," he had replied.

"I'm eating dinner at *Hawa's* house," *Adama* had continued, with the self-assured proclamation of a self-indulgent, old man.

Then I heard the fresh patter to my door of *Adama's* little bare feet.

"*Toubabou Hawa*, foreigner *Hawa*," my landlady *Korotum* said, with wisdom in her voice and softness in her eyes.

"White woman *Hawa*, *Adama* has become your son."

"Your shadow," the neighbor women exclaimed.

Korotum was a devout woman, but one who left little to chance. A woman strong in her Muslim faith, she performed her ablutions and prayed at the neighboring mosque five times every day. Her animist West African roots, however, were never buried very deep, and she was not above asking those traditional spirits for help.

We would never have snakes or thieves at our house, she told me once.

Because she had *medicine*, she said.

There in the corner of the entryway, up high, hung a bundle of dried, beige herbs tied carefully with a piece of old, grayed string. In a place where theft was rising, where deadly vipers are found in the drinking water wells, and dancing cobras make your house their own, that *medicine* had a big job to do.

Korotum was kind, and though she had no formal education, she was a wise woman. She was also a woman willing to open her mind to ways different from her own, as she did the day I cried for the little nine-year old who worked in *Korotum's* home.

Korotum's daughter, *Aseitou*, was a tall, willowy, carefree, and unusually irresponsible teenager who frequented the back alleys, made eyes at the men, skirted her chores, and abandoned her own infant daughter in the rutted and dusty street in front of my house. And she abused *Aramatu*, the family's young domestic girl. Unhappy with the labored pace of *Aramatu's* work, *Aseitou* punished and threatened in harsh tones and a sharp voice, until little *Aramatu* sobbed loudly one afternoon in deep, echoing wails. Soon after hearing the long, anguished cries, I began to cry too. And I then saw one more side of West African life.

In the mere blink of an eye and a rush of tears, I single-handedly turned the neighborhood upside down.

What was so horrific that I, a white woman, would cry? Korotum and my worried neighbors wanted to know, in a place where even young children resolutely hold back their tears. Distressed, upset, and ashamed that a foreigner would be driven to cry in their neighborhood, on their watch, in their home, they came hastily to see what was so terribly wrong. They talked, and I cried, unable to say a word. The night slowly grew dark. You could feel the weight of sadness hang heavy in the air.

La nuit porte des conseils, the French say. *The night brings advice.*

The sun rose early the following morning on a bright new day. In the fresh air, under the morning sun, *Korotum* and a neighbor came to my door.

"*Korotum* wants to talk," the neighbor explained.

"What you saw was wrong," my landlady said through her interlocutor, a young neighbor woman who spoke reasonable French.

"*Aramatu's* family entrusted her to me, to wash and cook and clean. They sent her to live with me, far from the safety of her own home. If the roles were different and she were my daughter, I would cry too, finding her treated such a way."

From that morning on, *Aramatu's* life changed. She still worked hard seven days a week. But the hours were not quite as long, the words were softer, *Aseitou* was not quite as demanding, the chores were not quite as tough.

Among the dust and the dirt of southern Mali I also learned about pride. The population was heart-wrenchingly poor and life was coated with bright, red clay, but the people were neat and they kept their clothes clean. Many foreigners, on the other hand, were blithely content in wrinkled attire, the *casual* look. Sometimes dirty, in clothes torn but not patched, the unkempt foreigners, the *Toubabous*, who could easily afford better, unknowingly brought embarrassment and shame on themselves and those they were around. Among the Malians, only a crazy person wears rags. Carefully dressed, the women and men of this poor West African country were a sight to behold. The men – lean, muscular, and fit, were handsome in traditional clothes with their straight posture, hardened bodies, and smooth, dark skin. Nothing, though, surpassed the striking beauty of a Malian woman standing dignified, standing erect, with a twisted head wrap of bright-colored cotton worn like a priceless crown of jewels.

I learned about pride in the poise of a little neighbor girl, standing straight and tall with her mother when finally she was considered responsible enough to carry her newborn brother on her own young back. She, herself, was three and a half years old. In a country where there is always another baby on the way, responsibility comes early. With her mother's blessing, little *Khadija* made a pledge that day to carry her brother's new life in her hands, on her broad shoulders and small back, to care for and protect him with a maturity far beyond her years.

In Mali I learned, too, about the burden, or the privilege, of the color of your skin.

"You will see what it means to be the minority," my father said when he learned of my Africa plans.

Raised in a homogenized community of light, white skin, I now stood out in a crowd. The one white face in a sea of black. *The rich one. The loose one. The Imperialist.* Alternately the object of envy, or contempt. As one man spat in my face, I learned the complexities of global politics and the volatility of pride. *Ameriki muso.* American woman, whose country snubs Africa and whose government bullies the poor, some I encountered believed.

I learned there were dollar signs tattooed on my forehead. There for everyone else to see, though they were invisible when *I* looked in the mirror. *Foreign woman. Rich woman.* I learned to bargain well.

Western woman. Loose woman. Object of carnal desire. An easy conquest for sex. "I want to *get to know you.* I want to *fuck* you. *You need a good man,*" said too many men who passed me on the street. The married man who lay down on my desk at work, insisting he should keep me warm at night. The middle finger rubbing the center of my palm in those otherwise-ever-so-polite handshakes. The knock on my door of a stranger in the night. I learned to sit and laugh with the children when the men were crass.

It was the middle of the cold, dry season when I decided to venture north, to visit the legendary city of *Tomboctou.* It is known to us in the

West as the middle of nowhere, the end of the road, the most remote place on earth. Mid-morning I boarded the *Malitas* flight. An unreliable old third- or fourth-hand, repainted, gray, military plane that sometimes flew and sometimes did not. Boarding through a big, flat door behind the belly, I felt a bit like Jonas being swallowed by the whale. The stained and discolored seats were lumpy and worn. The cabin was stuffy and hot. The air got thin as we rose, giving way to somersaults in my stomach and a shortness of breath. It was a time of uncertain security in the country's North, so I felt lucky to get to *Tomboctou* at all.

It is a place of legends, imagination, and dreams, this famous city in the sand. It is a place of salt caravans, French explorers, literary references. It is an ancient seat of higher learning, and a place of historical repute. *Tomboctou. Timbuktu.*

"It really exists?" people ask me.

Yes, I say.

It does, I add.

I was there.

"When you get off the plane, just ask for my father. Everyone knows him. Anyone can take you to his home."

We all want to think our father is famous, well-known, a very important man, I thought silently to myself, hoping I would at least find one person who could point me to his house. I had been invited to stay at the home of the *Haïdaras,* the kind and generous family of a neighbor and good friend of mine down south.

A camel caravan traversed the dunes as our plane approached. It moved slowly in a gracefully curved arc, casting gray shadows on the gold-beige dunes. The sky was clear. The sun was bright. And the tarmac was littered with sand. Shielding my eyes from the sun's glare, I looked about as I walked away from the plane. A handful of blue-turbaned boys and men clamored about, all wanting to be my new best friend. I walked off to the side where one quiet young man stood alone.

"A salaam aleykoum. Bonjour. Do you know *Daidie Haïdara?"* I asked.

"Oui, Madame." Yes, I do.

So sure, I had been that it would not be true, I did a double-take and I asked him the question again.

"Do you know where to find his house?" I continued.

Again he answered that he did. *Everyone did know this man,* it seemed.

"Will you please take me there? He's my friend."

Within minutes I was standing face to face with *Daidie Haïdara* himself. He was a straight, lean, gray-haired man with black-rimmed glasses, gentle eyes, a comfortable handshake, a soft smile.

The family compound was a quiet place. A walled courtyard with a two-story, flat-roofed, mud brick house, a big shade tree in the center of the yard, a small kitchen building, a few well-worn chairs in the shade of the tree. Everything was a khaki-beige except the green leaves on the tree and the light blue of the sky overhead. It was an oasis. A piece of solitude. A place of peace. It was a corner of life where I immediately felt at home.

Daidie was a gracious, intelligent, and visionary man. I had already heard much about him from my friend *Ousmane,* his son. In a country where few boys and fewer girls receive an education, *Daidie* had a well-used library in his house, stocked with books in French and in English that he, his sons, and his daughters had read. In a country where young girls are too readily pulled out of school, he insisted his children, both his boys *and* his girls, go to school and study hard. So they could study at night when the light was gone and the sky was dark, he had invested in gas-fed reading lamps. Those children are now doctors and lawyers and teachers. *Daidie* was a wise and honorable man, and in Mali, a man well ahead of his time.

Daidie, his wives, his daughter and sons welcomed me into their spacious home. They took me to walk on the dunes, to visit the sandy streets and the historic sites, the ancient seat of Islamic learning, the market, the flute maker, the bakery. We passed camels, *Tomboctou's* massive iron-studded, hand-carved wooden doors, and young boys selling matches and onions and imported bouillon cubes from crooked tables in the dusty, sun- and wind-faded streets. We drank bitter, sweet Arabic mint tea boiled over charcoal embers. At night we shared rice with a delicious leaf and vegetable stew accompanied by thick *Tomboctou* bread, far from the clamor and commotion of the tourist hotels.

Though I did not realize it at first, I was being seduced by the magic of the desert. By one of the earth's greatest stretches of sand. As the stars came out, *Daidie* took me up the ladder to his flat roof to show me the magnificent *Sahara* sky. One at a time, as we stood there quietly, the stars blinked as if to welcome me to this enchanted, faraway place.

"Could I sleep on the roof?" I asked.

Daidie paused for a moment under the stunning night sky.

"Will you be warm enough?" he asked with a look of fatherly concern.

"I have a sleeping bag and you've given me a thick woolen blanket. I should be warm enough."

There was another lengthy pause.

"Are you sure you want to?" he asked, again with a soft look on his face.

"It would be a special treat," I said. "Something I can't do back home."

"Let me get a second blanket and I'll help you bring your things."

There was magic glittering in those stars that night. There was peace in the diamond-studded sky. There was a gentleness in the soft breeze that caressed my face. I fell easily and quickly into a deep sleep, snug in my sleeping bag under two folded blankets in the crisp chill of the *Sahara* night air.

In the morning I awoke with the first light of dawn. It was a gentle awakening to a soft, quiet light that transformed the dark of night into a clear, blue sky. With a three hundred and sixty-degree view, I was on top of the world there at the end of the earth. I sat up and pulled my knees to my chin, and relished how lucky I am. *Tomboctou*. Few Americans even know it really exists. I was there.

When I began to hear the stirrings of life in the two floors and the courtyard down below, I climbed down the wooden ladder. There sat *Daidie* in a straight-back chair, just inside the ground floor door. He had a faded red blanket around his shoulders and a rifle across his lap. I realized then, that his concern the night before about whether I would be warm, was in fact about whether I would be safe. The rebels had recently made violent and unpredictable forays into town in the dark of night, raiding houses, stealing vehicles, leaving people tied up in a tangle of ropes. *Daidie* did not have the heart to say *no* when I wanted to sleep on his roof, but nor had he the peace of mind to sleep that night with me bedded down under my blanket of stars. He sat up and silently kept watch at his door so I, his guest, could enjoy the wonders of the desert and the gift of a most precious night on his roof.

Much later and back in *Bamako*, the night was warm but I had been unusually, overwhelmingly, inexplicably tired all day. Suddenly and without warning around seven p.m., the telltale chills began, uncontrolled shivers and a cold that blankets could not relieve, a headache commenced and I soon threw up. Once again, I had fallen ill in a routine I came in West Africa to know too well. This time it was malaria. Though I had been raised on tales of its rampage in my own father's blood, until that night I had beaten the malaria odds. One bite of an infected mosquito is all it takes, though, and my turn, too, had come. In a vain attempt to quiet the fire that was starting to burn, I took aspirin for the fever and suffered badly through the night. It was unusual that I was so very frightfully sick. Fortunate that I was in a small French-owned hotel, I dragged myself downstairs when the morning came. *Could they direct me to the French-owned clinic in the center of town?* I asked, bone-weary, nauseated, and scalding hot.

"We have a Romanian doctor here in the hotel right now. Why don't you consult her first?"

A few brief questions, a simple blood test, and one good look at me brought out the big guns of Western medicine. Two injections, four imported French pills, and a firm directive to return to bed, as if I had the strength to do anything else. *Madame Médecin,* the doctor, followed me to my room, accompanied by her Malian nurse. Within moments I was again flat on my back, an intravenous drip of more drugs running swiftly into my arm.

For two days I stayed tied to the mosquito net that pulled double duty to suspend my *IV* drip, but I was too worn, too sick, and too weak to care. I was, no doubt, a sad and comical sight, lying hostage to that sheer white net while war raged in my body against this microscopic but all too often deadly bug. This parasite that invades your blood and can too easily infect your brain. I had already lost two people I knew to the scourge that drains the strength, the economy, the will of much of the African continent. But eventually I awoke from my malaria-induced fog and found the sun was shining and life was good once again. The doctor removed my *IV*. I had new energy and kick. My health was back. I was once again well and free. Able to afford proper medicine and good care, I was one of the lucky ones.

Despite the dysentery, the malaria, the incessant demands for clothes and jewelry and money and sex, life was good to me in Mali. All good things must come to an end, though. I would look back many times on those years with fondness and warmth, but the seasons changed, the children grew, and for me it was time to move on. There is a saying in Mali. *If you set foot in one hundred lands, you can sit with the wise, old men.* What first compelled me to travel there eventually drove me to continue on. Blessed as I was by Mali's friendship and culture, laughter and warmth, it was time to leave. Africa had set the stage, but my feet had grown restless. Mali had become my school, but there were more classrooms, more countries in my future, more people to meet, more lands and cultures to explore.

Somewhere, the old men were waiting. It was time for me to go.

If I Had Only Known

Tajikistan (1995)

Perhaps he knew, as I did not,
that the world was made round
so we would not see too far down the road.

Out of Africa, a Sydney Pollack film

I t was madness on that overcrowded international flight. Five hours of bedlam and nerves as the dilapidated old *Tajik Air* plane hurled me through the skies. It was a flying machine held together with chewing gum, chicken wire, and string; it was a sardine can with wings, hand-me down transport that tested my faith. Five long hours. Animals and children aboard, women, and men. The clatter of Russian and *Farsi.* The smell of hot tea. Black hair. Neon-bright clothes in a vivid clash of fuchsia, emerald, marigold, white, black, and royal blue. Ruddy cheeks, richly embroidered prayer caps, gold-capped teeth. The luggage bins overflowed but no one cared. *A seat belt missing?* So what. *Put the dog in a muzzle?* Why bother? *How many more passengers could sit in the aisle?* In this part of the world, planes are expensive but life is cheap. We flew south from Moscow on a wing and a prayer.

The sun was strong and the air was stifling. We arrived in the chaos and searing heat of a broken-down airport on a Central Asian midsummer day. The air was parched. The terminal was in disarray. A rush of baggage, people, machine guns, strange words, strange letters, and bright, bright sun greeted me then exploded in my head. I looked about.

The noise was deafening. The floor was dirty. The place was an unkempt, chaotic mess. The world around me quickly became little more than an insanely colorful blur.

Did I see the mountains? How could I miss? Some of the highest peaks in the world, they dwarfed all else around. What about the muted orange, blue, and gold murals on the two tall buildings up ahead? And the shadowy blood-stained pedestrian underpass?

"That's where people were shot just a few months ago in the height of the war," the person who had collected me at the airport cheerfully said, in that weird state of mind that sets in when you have lost your perspective because you have seen far too much.

"*Malakum,*" I heard piercing the still morning air.

"*Malakum,*" she called in a sing-song voice.

Fresh milk for sale.

What hour in the morning was it? Five o'clock? Six? Fresh milk?

"*Malakum.*"

Lady, be quiet. Go home and let me sleep. I was exhausted. We had just arrived the day before. I had been so tired in Moscow after three days of no sleep and a crowded, filthy plane from New York, I had fallen asleep in a cab.

"*Maa-laa-kum.*"

Would she please go away? Wondering what had compelled me to travel from the safety of San Francisco to this war-ravaged corner of the earth, I grudgingly crawled from my bed. The maple-colored hardwood floor, smooth and cool to my bare feet, was little consolation for the interruption of my much-needed sleep. I felt faint, overwhelmed by a deep fatigue that reached clear through my bones.

The apartment was lovely. It sat on a broad, tree-lined street. Beautifully furnished with mahogany, lace curtains, and crystal chandeliers. Little did it matter that aluminum foil overrode the electrical circuit breakers. Little did it matter that we fried all but one of the electrical sockets, that the phone was tapped, the maid stole our cooking oil, burned our sweaters, and ruined our clothes. The apartment was a luxury, even if a life-sized, full-color photo of a tropical palm-lined beach covered the entire surface of one otherwise very elegant living room wall. What momentary lapse of decorating taste had led the owner to that? Time and again, I would shake my head in wonder, and laugh as at least it gave me some brief, comic relief in a dire place in a tragic time. Once undoubtedly an enviable prize, by now the apartment was a testimony to much that failed after the Soviet Union dissolved.

On far too many occasions the electrical wires in our building overheated; they reached a dangerous, odiferous, white -hot glow with great regularity. Too often the water did not run, the gas went dry, or the electricity did not work; sometimes they *all* stopped for days on end. We kept a bevy of buckets in the bathroom, filled to the brim, just for those many occasions the tap went dry. And we hoped the immersion heater would not electrocute us when we tried to take the winter chill off our frigid bath water.

One Saturday afternoon, Annabel and I both smelled smoke though there were no signs of fire in the neighborhood. Eventually, in a very sober moment, we realized the hot, burning smell was coming from beneath our living room floor. The Iranian Ambassador and his family who lived downstairs were gone for the day, their apartment locked tight.

What to do in a place where things did not work and fire departments did not exist? We left too, for much of the rest of the day, our passports and cash in hand. We drove around town for hours before we returned, wondering all the while whether our apartment and our belongings had burned to the ground.

We had settled quietly in the center of town, Annabel and I. We had met in a taxi just one day before, picked up by the same driver en route to the airport in Moscow for the same flight south. There was comfort in a strange place from the company of someone who speaks the same language as you. Sharing an apartment was a wise move. Far more experienced at the time, with such places than me, it was Annabel who brought my spirits back up when in frustration or fear they slipped very low. It was Annabel who gave me courage when life was dark. It was Annabel who made me laugh, on whose shoulder I could cry. A New Zealand *Kiwi* with a quick wit, a joyous laugh, the conviction of a saint, and a heart of gold, I owe much to this new-found friend.

Only a month before, I had not heard of Tajikistan. Now on an assignment to develop women-owned businesses in a war-ravaged region down south, I was supposed to live in *Dushanbe* for a year.

Post-Soviet Central Asia. *Tajikistan.* The frontier. The Wild, Wild West. A baking inferno in summer, it was bitter, bitter cold once winter set in. *What had I thought? Had some West African parasite compromised my brain?* Again I had committed a part of my life to a place that was foreign, a people I did not know, and a need far greater than any relief I could possibly bring. *Tajikistan.* It was always a country that faced harsh times. Now, post-*USSR*, it was very desperately poor and wracked with a complicated civil war that left houses shelled, shelves bare, women widowed, and children with little more than ragged clothes, an empty stomach, and a gray, suspicious stare.

Tajikistan. It was a country that would try my compassion, raise my fear, amaze me, educate me, and reduce me to tears. It would make me smile. It would make me cry. More than once I threatened with great seriousness to ride out on a four-legged yak, scheduled air flights being unreliably few and unpredictably far between. This country would build my strength but play games with my head. It was a country that would steal my illusions, try my nerves, test my resolve, but give me the precious gift of a very dear friend. *That which does not kill you makes you stronger*, it has been said. Oh how very, very true.

The days were long and the nights were short. Nothing could have prepared me for what lay ahead. Petty theft was common. The banks had no money. The soldiers were drunk. Fuel supplies ran low but testosterone ran very, very high. Though the merchants sold twenty brands of vodka they had only a few bars of soap. On a good day, the mountains took your breath away and the melons kissed your lips. Murders were brutal. Clothes were bright. Smiles were rare. I thought I had seen it all in Mali, one of the poorest countries in the world. But I had not even come close. This was the 1990s in Tajikistan.

The summer was filled with a blistering heat but in December I felt a penetrating cold whose intensity flooded my bones with a brutal, soul-shattering chill I would have never thought possible from the warmth of my very distant American home. The snow fell, the temperatures plummeted, the gas ran out, and the electricity failed. Cold weather. Cold water. Cold food. A cold bed. Bitter, *bitter* cold with no relief, no way to get warm. During the day I stood outside in the miniature patches of sun to feel just an infinitesimal bit of warmth. In the dark I slept in flannel pajamas and socks in a sleeping bag under two blankets and a quilt. Never again, even in Iraq at one hundred thirty-six degrees, would I complain about baking, stifling, sweltering heat.

"*A salaam aleykoum. Wa aleykoum salaam. Shumo nargs asted? Tashakor, man nargs astam. Shumo machina benzene pul ast?*"

"Hello. How are you? Thank you, I'm fine. Does your car have a full tank of gas?"

After months of tutoring, these are the only words of Tajik or *Farsi* I can now recall. Few in number, these words speak volumes about the new priorities in my life. Buying gasoline, such a simple affair we took for granted in the West, was a challenge at best, illegal most of the time, and always a matter of personal safety. If what my drivers told me was straight, often the only place you could buy gasoline was behind someone's house, the house of someone you needed to intimately trust. There, and usually only there, could you buy fuel. From someone who knew someone who had stolen it. *From the Army.* To run out of gas in *Dushanbe* was one thing; you could always walk home. To run out in the field, where bullets still flew, animosities still raged, vindictiveness reigned, and vigilantes ruled, was something I did not want to test.

"Are you *sure* your car has a full tank of gas?"

I often went south to the Afghan border where the civil war had been the worst. It was a desolate place where the earth was parched and cracked, the houses had been shelled, and the men had disappeared,

41

having left to fight, having been killed, or having fled the villages in fear. Mistrust was rife; ethnic tensions ran strong. The land was harsh and the children wore rags. But it was a place rich in culture with an enduring hospitality and a deep sense of pride.

Few men remained in villages torn apart by war. *Fight or flight.* They were conscripted, joined the army, ran off, or died in the fray. Only the old men, the injured, the infirm had stayed at home, leaving a whole generation of women to care, alone, for the elderly and the kids. Women, most of whom had never been allowed from their homes. These were strong women; they were brave women. But sheltered as they had been, they were ill-prepared for what life brought. Women who had no formal job skills had six or eight or ten hungry mouths to feed. Women in their thirties, their forties, their fifties had not once been to a local market but now had to earn money, now had to learn how to publicly buy and sell. Unfathomable to me as a Western woman who travels the globe alone, the world her oyster shell, I learned about boundaries and barriers culturally imposed. I learned about the luxury, or lack, of choice. I learned about freedom of movement. I learned about being allowed to take my destiny in my own hands. Or not, as I, or someone else, so choose. I learned that just a simple village market a kilometer or two from their homes had long been beyond these women's reach, a place forbidden by the men in their lives, their fathers, their husbands, their brothers, their sons, the village elders, the religious chiefs. To me it was an incomprehensible tragedy beyond words, but one that allowed no time for sentiment as the children went to bed hungry at night.

Tajikistan. Central Asia. The hospitality is legendary. These women raised their children in the broken carcasses of very modest homes. But these widows who struggled to put scraps of food on their table and clothes on their kids sent their children scurrying next door and around the corner at the first sign of my approach. Running to the neighbors to see who had what. Sugar? Fresh bread? Mulberries? Dried fruit, or nuts? Maybe a tiny scrap of meat. A hot kettle of watery soup? In moments our hostess laid out a gracious spread. Soup, nuts, bread, fruit. Despite our pleading, they never stopped. Women whose cupboards were empty. Whose babies were barefoot. Whose eyes were hollow. Whose children no longer laugh. These villagers who were so desperately poor could not bear the shame of failing to offer a foreigner *tea*. With big smiles and outstretched arms they welcomed us to their homes. They broke my heart as they warmed my soul. From these women I learned about selfless giving and strength from pride. *Would I, in their circumstances, be as generous and kind?* Time and again in the developing world I would see that those who have the very least invariably give others the most.

Though the earth was khaki and gray, the cloudless sky just a faint, sun-bleached blue, and the life was tenuous, restricted, and hard, these women expressed a ruggedly defiant passion in the colorful clothing they wore. They may have been constrained by the circumstances of their birth or the dictates of men but a strong spirit coursed through these women's veins and erupted in the blinding fuchsia, bright green, bright blue, and bright yellow-gold stripes and diamonds of the traditional *ikat* fabrics they wore. Vibrant waves of rich color undulated across their loose, shapeless dresses and baggy pants while sparkling gold capped their teeth.

In the afternoons the women, with their brilliant clothing, braids that reached clear down to their hips, and interminable, unending chores, stayed at home while old men with grayed beards and sad eyes took me out to show me their crops and their herds and their fields. Dressed handsomely in the manner of an earlier time, the men wore frayed, faded, quilted cotton *chappan* robes belted at the waist by a colorful silk scarf in a neat triangular fold, its tip pointing down to the ground. There between the melons and vines and dry soil, these weathered, old men led me out under the burning sun. Elegantly twisted turbans in muted colors of burgundy, teal, copper, and green crowned their heads above bushy, unkempt brows. Deep furrows lined their tanned and bearded faces; their hobbled walk and the worn, tired look of their scuffed black leather boots told of a difficult life in a land that gives less easily than it takes away. There in the parched fields under the scorching sun, they talked of the goats giving birth, of succulent red pomegranates, of rich almonds and sweet apricots, of the hopes and dreams they followed but would never reach. There, too, they shared with me straight from the vine, the unforgettable gift of the sweetest melons the world has known.

Insecurity in Tajikistan at that time was a constant worry; it was always a serious concern. On more than one occasion there were military skirmishes in the region where I worked down south. If things had turned really ugly, it would have been nearly impossible for me to get out of the country, or even just into or out of town. With that as my backdrop, my heart did flips late one day when an army tank appeared just as our vehicle came to the crest of a hill more than an hour outside of town. Its gun was pointed right at our car. Authorities said the war was over but someone had forgotten to tell those who fought. An opposing tank was not far behind us, and I could only hope we would pass before the two drew fire.

Not long after, I had a sad, dark, disconcerting sort of night. The kind that begs questions without answers. The kind where you suddenly feel you've slipped, unwittingly, into some dark and bottomless abyss. At somewhere past midnight I awoke out of a deep sleep to hear the crackle of two-way radios, the black shadows of a frantic voice, and words that make your muscles tense and your stomach knot.

"*What do we do?*" the black two-way radio on my nightstand asked in a sound of panic that filled my darkened room.

What do we do with the body? What do we do? Do we bring the body back to Dushanbe? the distant voice in the middle of the night implored.

The *United Nations Military Observers to Tajikistan* had been brokering peace talks. It was a mammoth task at a very difficult time. In the flash of a gun that night one man paid the ultimate price. An *UNMOT* officer shuttling between the two sides was killed, murdered in cold blood at close range, by a man in whom he had placed his trust. Watching his fellow officers load his casket a few days later into the back of a United Nations plane left a cold pit in my stomach that I will not easily forget.

Though it hit me with the convulsing force of an electric shock, in retrospect it was no real surprise when one morning the army tanks rolled through the center of town. Alone in the apartment, I awoke early that late September day. Feeling agitated for reasons I cannot explain, I gave in, got up, and started to get ready for work. I went to the kitchen for a glass of water, but returned to my bedroom having drunk only a sip. All seemed routine until I heard a loud, explosive *bang* and the distinctive, unmistakable sound of shattering glass. Gunfire? A *Molotov* cocktail? A very forcefully propelled rock? Adrenalin drilled through my veins as I listened intently for more. It seemed like hours though only a minute or maybe two could really have passed as a variety of scattered thoughts raced through my head.

But there was nothing more. No noise. No clangor. No unusual activity to discern. I held my breath momentarily and waited, not wanting to miss some small auditory clue for the simple sound of my own breath. The new silence weighed heavy on me like a jacket of lead. No birds sang. No determined woman called out to sell fresh milk. No dogs barked. The seconds and the minutes stood still in a vacuum. The clock may as well have stopped.

I had no idea what had just happened, or why, but I wanted to know. This sort of thing was new to me but I believed the sooner I knew the problem the better off I would be. Knowledge is power, especially when things go wrong. Slowly and quietly I walked from my bedroom one careful, deliberate, tentative step at a time. As I tiptoed to the living room. I held my breath. My bones knocked against each other, and my knees shook hard.

No broken windows in the living room.

I slipped quietly to the hall.

No broken glass there.

No smell of smoke, no crackle of flames that I could discern.

45

I went toward the kitchen. In infinitely slow motion I turned and I peered inside.......

What the hell?

The porch windows were unbroken. The kitchen windows were fine. The porch door was still closed, its glass panes still intact. But the green linoleum-covered floor was newly littered with debris. That ordinary glass of water I had drunk from just minutes before now lay in glistening shards on the floor. A knife that had been next to it on the counter was on the floor too, now six very long feet away. Other small things that had been nearby now lay strewn about. I swallowed my heart and looked around, feeling as if I had been transported to outer space.

"Poltergeist?" my sister would later ask when I recounted what I saw.

A million unanswered questions charged like a freight train through my mind. I slipped back to the bedroom. I finished putting on my clothes. I left the glass where it lay, exited the apartment, triple-locked the door, and walked next door to my office to bury myself in my work. I did not *really* need breakfast, and *Ludi*, our wily, way under-worked, way over-paid maid, could clean up the mess on the floor.

While my heart continued to race the morning marched forward in yet another new, unexpected, unsettling way. Having gone to work so early, I had been alone in the office for two hours when a low, guttural noise rolled over the nearby regiment of trees. I was still jittery from the exploding glass.

I walked to the windows, trying to peer through the breaks in the leaves of the trees that lined the elegant street where we lived. My breath caught on a hook in my throat as I caught sight of what paraded by. There in front of my office and my apartment was something I had previously seen only on TV screens airing the nightly news, watched from the safety of a living room continents away from where the televised events were actually taking place.

There, before my eyes, a column of drab green army tanks rumbled past me with their guns pointed at forty-five degrees as their tracks rolled down the street. Until then I did not believe in any religion, but at that moment I was tempted to start.

Strange things happened in *Dushanbe*. A lot of odd and very disconcerting things. As if the *UNMOT* shooting, the breaking glass, the army tanks, and a mid-afternoon car-jacking of the vehicle next to mine were not enough, I awoke with a start one night, to bright flashes of light, sizzling, loud pops, and a heart-stopping *bang*. My heart leaped from my chest as sparks shot from the ceiling light directly above my head. There in my bedroom in the pitch-black dark of night, I held the ringside seat to a first-class fireworks show. Not brought about by some hormone-charged writhing fit of late night passion, but the faulty wiring of the elegant crystal chandelier hanging directly overhead. *Sweet Jesus*, I thought, *get me through these days and these nights*.

And then, there was *Valentina*. A middle-aged, shapely, bleached-blond Russian masseuse recommended by an expatriate colleague and friend. She worked in an upstairs room of a mostly abandoned, multi-story office complex. The building was uncomfortably empty in a lonely, disturbingly desolate part of town, but it seemed everyone who worked in an office worked in a dark room of a run-down section in a dingy building that made me pause. In *Dushanbe* this was nothing new. In this place at that time, most buildings were awfully dismal and depressingly gray, with grime in their shadowy corners, and dark halls that echoed a hollow sound when you walked. Trusting my colleague and hoping to relieve a mountain of accumulated stress, I had tracked *Valentina* down. *She gives a good massage*, this expatriate woman had said. With very few alternatives around, I overlooked the venue and decided to give her a try.

"Swedish? Athletic?..........Erotic?" *Valentina* asked, with a cool voice but a sly, seductive smile and a clearly discernable twinkle in her eye.

Erotic?

Thank you, but the ordinary Swedish type would be just fine, I said.

A palpable disappointment crossed *Valentina's* face, but a good solid work-over of tense muscles was all that I sought right then. Things were a little crazy in this rather dysfunctional place but at that moment, I *just* wanted an ordinary massage. Simply the old-fashioned kind that loosens the tension and softens the knots in shoulder muscles far too tight from the rigors of fear-laced, adrenalin-charged everyday life. Just when once again I mistakenly thought I had seen it all, *Valentina*, the well-recommended masseuse, wanted to show me more.

To travel is to learn, and in Tajikistan most lessons were depressingly, frighteningly, uncomfortably hard. I learned about cultural barriers that work to keep women dependent and poor. I learned about Conservatism's dark side in the fate of three women hanged *for adultery*, the villagers said. More likely a trumped-up charge to cover the hatred of a different ethnicity, some man's errant behavior or wandering eye, or the jealousy of a woman scorned. A tragically, unjustifiably high price to pay, whatever the reason.

I also learned about hatred in the local market one day, right between the potatoes and the cheese and the fruit. Boiling, blinding hatred. The kind that eats the soul, poisons the spirit, destroys humanity, and drives too many people to wantonly kill. When I close my eyes, I can still see the steel in the ice-cold eyes of an adolescent boy, maybe fourteen years of age. I can still see the swift, deliberate motion of his hand. His straight fingers sliced across his neck like a butcher's knife as he faced Annabel and looked her straight in the eye, telling her in the flash of his hand that he wanted to slit her throat. What distills such cold, hard hatred in people I cannot begin to know, especially in someone so young.

I saw Tajikistan's dark side but I experienced its stellar, breathtaking beauty as well. Traveling by four-wheel drive vehicle to the far North, I had the extraordinary privilege of crossing some of the world's highest mountains. Mountains so steep rock slides regularly bury whole towns, so high a pass we crossed stood at twenty thousand feet, the driver said.

Mountains with ridges as sharp as the blade of a knife. Their beauty was regal, their power was alive.

The road we took was not for the faint of heart. It was not for those with a low tolerance for risk. More than once we had barely one lane to travel where gravity had greedily sucked most of the roadbed away. As we rounded dangerously ice-slicked hairpin curves in the mid-October day, I looked down. Way, way down at the tiny world below. Houses were barely a dot, roads just a whisper-thin, winding thread. We passed small villages a million miles from nowhere and I could only wonder how their inhabitants survive. The views were stunning but beauty in such a distant and remote place rarely puts food on the table and clothes on your back.

Life was hard in Tajikistan, but some spirits ran heartwarmingly deep. *Abdul Rashid* was a lean and lively, middle-aged man with thick, wavy salt-and-pepper hair, a broad mustache, and the dance of mischief in his eyes. He had an optimistic song in his heart and perpetual rhythm in his feet. When music broke out, as it occasionally did, *Abdul Rashid* morphed into a new, decades-younger man. He was instantly rejuvenated; he was immediately reborn. He let go of his worries. His eyes lit up. The hollows of his chiseled cheeks filled out. The edges of his ready smile curved upward several degrees, and his arms reached out straight to the sides to twist and to turn with the rhythm of that Eastern, oriental way the Tajiks dance. When the music began, nothing could quiet the twinkle in his eye. And nothing, oh nothing, could keep his feet still. If this man had his way, we would all dance our way through life, and he would undoubtedly take the lead.

And there was kind, gentle *Iskandar*. He was a ruggedly good-looking man with dark hair, inquiring, penetrating eyes the rich color of coffee and a perennial late afternoon shadow on his broad cheeks and firm chin. He had a quiet, pensive air; his eyes were thoughtful, his smile was warm, and his heart was good. He was one of only three individuals in the country who I thought might help me if things got really bad and I needed to flee quickly on a moment's notice. Late one blue, pre-

49

Christmas day, *Iskandar* gave me a treasured gift by making me laugh when in frustration and fatigue I wanted to cry. With three words of English, animated gestures, and the rudimentary Russian he knew I could barely understand, he asked with great passion and effort and concern whether I believed in Santa Claus, where I would be for Christmas, and what I would do when I went home. In that land of broken promises and rampant mistrust, *Iskandar* believed in Santa Claus, and hoped I would be home for Christmas with my family, he said.

I had some of my darkest overseas moments in Tajikistan, that distant, god-forsaken Central Asian place, but I also had some of life's best. When I think of the adolescent boy in the market my nerves tighten. I clench my jaw when I think of the children with their dirty, matted hair and ragged clothes, standing barefoot in the snow. When I think of the three women who were hanged, I ask myself where justice is, why humanity has gone absent, why it has taken such a break. But when I think of those women offering me tea when they really had none, my eyes soften and my heart cries. Such was my time in that tiny, forgotten, forsaken, impoverished corner of the world. An amalgam of sweetness, fear, and grief. Of tension and stress, of laughter, and gratitude, and tears.

I experienced in Tajikistan that which taught me lessons I would not have sought if I had been able to see what the future held. I came as one person in June and in December I left as another. Hardened, softened, humbled, and strengthened by that which I had seen and experienced. Had I been able to see around the corner, had I known what lay ahead in Tajikistan before I boarded that overloaded plane, I would most assuredly not have gone. But today I am richer in spirit, I am wiser, and I am stronger in life for it all. Precisely because I could not see too far ahead, too far around the curve, too far down the road, too far over the hill, I ultimately saw, and learned much, much more.

Had I been able to see ahead, I would not have gone but I would not have learned what Tajikistan would teach, I would not have grown. Yes, indeed. There is a good reason why *the world is round.*

A Strong Stomach and a Good Sense of Humor

India (1996)

*The most important things to take when you travel
are a strong stomach and a good sense of humor.*

Ambassador Peggy Blackford

He was a skinny little man with small black eyes and a rather prominent hooked nose. His white shirt was grayed and the collar was stained. His clothes fit loosely; they were at least two full sizes too large. He sat alone in a boring moment at a tedious job, a dull expression asleep on his face. His eyes moved upward slightly in a half-hearted effort to meet mine as I spoke.

"I'd like to change one hundred-fifty U.S. dollars," I said at three in the morning to the teller at the exchange window of the airport office of the official *State Bank*.

The fluorescent light took on a thin yellow cast through its discolored plastic case. The counter was worn. The floor tiles needed a good scrub with hot water, steel wool, and bleach. The agent took my money and wiggled his head back and forth in a smooth horizontal figure eight I would see time and again over the coming several weeks. His thin hand reached down machine-like then came back up. He slapped a thick stack of dirty bills within my reach, then he slid me a grease-stained receipt. My fingers recoiled as I clasped the stack and began to count. Worn, tattered bills so grimy they reeked of rancid oil, filth, and dead fish. Just the thought of touching them made my nerves involuntarily repulse. *Twenty, twenty-one….ninety-eight, ninety-nine…one hundred and thirty-two. Wait a minute. I must have lost count.* It should have been more. I was tired, very tired, and the hour was very late. *Start over again. Sixty-nine, seventy,…eighty-eight, eight-nine,….once* more *one hundred thirty-two.* With this many bills, what are the odds of counting the same wrong number twice?

The little man with the weasel eyes, bad teeth, hunched back, and hollow chest sat still, a vacant look on his face.

"Excuse me, sir, but I would like you to count. I believe the amount of money you gave me is wrong."

I started to hand back the stack.

Without changing his expression, without as much as the blink of an eye, without a word crossing his lips, the bank teller's bony hand mechanically reached back down as if he had done this a thousand times, and perhaps he had. From under the tired and discolored counter he brought out a small stack of bills and pushed it my way. I counted it. Just the right number to properly complete my exchange. Three hundred *rupees.* The price of a three-hundred kilometer ride in an air-conditioned second class train. Easily more than the cost of several days' food, or a child's new set of clothes. Such was my introduction to the grinding poverty in India, where entire families live for generations in the remnants of a cardboard box. Where some city dwellers are born, live, and die never setting foot in a house, while the sons and daughters of the very elite, raised by servants and educated at the best schools money can buy, drip in gold and exquisite jewels as they enjoy cocktails from the world's best whiskey, or drink the finest wine.

As I made my way out of the Arrivals hall into the darkness of the remaining night, I glanced about. Beggars in tattered rags lined my way, calling out with a single, desperate voice and a sad look in their eyes. I continued toward a group of taxis, preparing my mind for what was to be a desolate and lonely ride into town. The sweet, acrid smell of burning *hashish* hung heavy in the chill of the early morning air. *Was my cab driver high?* I asked myself as we sped off, just the two of us, into the black *Delhi* night. I wasn't sure. *Was he honest?* I wondered but would never really know. *Would he get me to my desired destination safely?* Yes, that he did. In the end, it was all that mattered as I left the airport's seamier side for the comfort of a clean hotel.

After a warm shower I fell into a deep sleep between the smooth sheets of a soft bed in a quiet room. When I awoke, I purchased a bus ticket and got on my way. There were places to go, things to do, people to see. And now, before me in the warm afternoon sun of a cool February day stood the regal *Taj Mahal*, one of the great beauties of the world, the architectural gem of India, a timeless testimony to the tremendous love of a rich man for his late wife. The great *Taj Mahal*. A model of symmetry, craftsmanship, engineering, affection, and grace. An ornamental wonder that no photo does justice and no words can adequately describe. It was a deeply inspiring start for a cross-country India trek.

After touring the *Taj* and walking its grounds, I went to the station and boarded a bus, a red-colored 'semi-deluxe.' A worn-out, beaten-up old clunker that rivaled the worst I rode in Africa. The driver was a scrawny man who had not seen a good meal in years but he seemed a friendly sort. His eyes and hair were black as coal, his skin a soft cinnamon brown. He was also serious about business so we departed on time, sputtering forth into the log-jam of cacophonous traffic and noxious blue fumes. I was the one light-skinned foreigner among a crowd, looking well out of place among the strong arms and tanned faces that carried boundless worries and heavy loads. While I traveled lightly out of luxury of leisure time and relative wealth, my companions traveled under hardship and out of commanding social duty and economic need. I could imagine faraway places with unpronounceable names and make my dreams come true. They agonized about debts to parents, hungry children, falling houses, and the weighty burden of daily life.

For the better part of a day we rattled down the road, passing hour after hour of golden-flowered mustard fields, scores of monkeys the color of a cup of strong tea, laboring ox carts, a tree full of broad-shouldered vultures with long, thick beaks, hungry stomachs, and sinister eyes. We passed camels, buffalo, wild dogs, and *sari'd* women with urns of priceless water or loads of firewood balanced precariously atop their heads. The sky was light and the air was fresh. February was a good time of year.

When we finally arrived, I tumbled out of the bus, my legs weak from hours of holding my backpack on my tired knees. The bus station was a noisy, dusty, crowded, and chaotic slice of life that smelled of diesel fumes, curry, urine, and sweat. I made my way out and continued by foot, dodging those who wanted to carry my bag or *be my friend*. Quickly I checked into a hotel, dropped my things, and went back out; there were markets, palaces, restaurants, temples, shops, and streets to explore.

At its very core, India inundates, saturates, overwhelms your senses with a plethora of sights, sounds, textures, tastes, and smells of the extremes of its everyday life. The brilliant *saris* and silks light the world afire. The marigold garlands seem to burst into flame. The smooth feel of a cool yogurt *lassi* soothes your tongue and caresses your throat while the grit of the path scratches your eyes and grinds under your feet. The wandering hand grabs your buttocks, as countless bodies press tightly against yours. The music enchants; the movies entertain. The chili burns your mouth and the smell of curry tickles your nose while the odors of filth make your stomach churn. *The good, the bad, and the ugly*. In India there is no escape. Haunting music floats over your ears. Incense burns. Merchants vie for your cash. Beggars squat on the ground. Children squeal and babies cry. The flood of stimuli assaults your body and your brain as it invades your every cell with an intensity unheard of almost anywhere else. *That* was the India I found.

Everywhere I turned there were temples, as varied as they were abundant, each one the work of architects and craftsmen creatively, artistically inclined. Some were gaily colored in elaborate bouquets of rose, yellow, mint, peach, and baby blue; others were the quiet, meditative color of sand. Many were modest, some were grand. One notable group sported *Kama Sutra* sex positions carved in graphic, three-dimensional relief, a veritable how-to guide. A few were simple and plain. At some, flesh burned at the riverside *Ghats* as families cremated their dead. At most, pilgrims prostrated in religious devotion, lowering themselves close to the ground. The *sadhus* intrigued me though they simultaneously gave me the chills. The piercing eyes and the long, greasy hair of these aesthetic religious men had a disheveled, almost demonic quality; their naked contortionist frames all painted in ghostly white looked unnatural, unholy, strikingly chilling, and odd. *It is a bizarre life they lead*, I thought silently to myself, as they stood on their heads and tied their lean bodies, like rubber, into knots.

Elsewhere, the markets buzzed with commerce. Everything imaginable was available for sale. Cheap perfumes and strong incense, jewelry, and paper, spices, and fabrics, and food. Truck parts, school books, music cassettes, and no doubt much out of sight that I prefer not to see. The stalls were packed to the brim with all manner of goods and the streets were teeming with an expansive assortment of women and children and animals and men. Shoppers, snake charmers, beggars, and saints. The uneven pathway was littered with rocks, and rubbish, and mud. Empty, open space has no place in the crowded Indian bazaar.

In the market's food section the smell of cooked vegetables and curry surfed the air. It rode in rich waves over and around the pedestrians who pushed their way through the crowd. Teased by the fragrant notes of Indian cuisine, my mouth watered at the mere thought of a meal. An intense, inspired, spicy-hot blend of flavors whets your appetite, drains your sinuses, waters your eyes, and burns your throat. With zest and imagination Indian cuisine lights sparklers that dance on your tongue. Warm curries, colorful rice. Pink carrots. Smooth *dhal.* Green peas and white *paneer.* Crisp *pappodums*, soft *naan.* Cardamom, chili, ginger, turmeric, mustard, allspice, star anise, and cumin. Indian kitchens combine an infinite assortment of vegetables and spice in a delicate balance that transforms ordinary vegetables into one of the most intricately imaginative and varied cuisines in the world, surpassed by none and rivaled by few. It is not for the timid stomach or the sensitive tongue, but it is a limitless treasure for the adventurous gastronomic soul.

Unquestionably for me, the fabrics market was the best. It was a brilliant kaleidoscope of colors. Peacock, saffron, emerald, and ruby painted this world. Burgundy, burnt gold, olive, and teal. Metallic threads and bits of mirror. Stacks of bolts of exquisite cloth. Patchwork. Embroideries, delicate, and bold. Paisleys, block prints, *Damask*, sateen. Whispery cottons and lustrous silks. From these fabrics, the Indian women are the most beautifully dressed on earth. Were *I* to attempt to walk in a *sari*, I would undoubtedly leave an embarrassing trail of fine billowing cloth in my wake. But these women glide like a wisp of smoke through a crowd with an ease that no runway model in Europe can possibly match; and every inch of *their saris* remains in place. With their *kohl*-rimmed eyes and their glossy black hair, these beauties exude mystery and charm that drives envy in women and turns weak-kneed the men.

The cool February air gave way to a blazing heat as the weeks passed and I went deep into the far corners of *Rajasthan*. Soon my body fell into a quiet trance from the soft rhythm of a camel's stride as he lumbered across the khaki-gray gravel and sand. For three days I reveled in solitude and bliss, when time stood still in the dry expanse of the *Thar* Desert. By day we crossed the scorched earth. By night we slept on a bed of sand, wrapped in heavy blankets against the cold desert night, guarded by a sentry of stars that glistened like tiny bits of scattered glass. *Prabhu,* my camel-driver and guide, was an old man; his face was deeply lined and his hair had gone gray. His jacket was khaki-colored wool. His turban of gauze was white. The edges of his pants were frayed and his brown sandals worn. His eyes were gentle, his voice was soft. He spoke no English but well-schooled over a lifetime in the ways of the desert, he gave a quiet confidence that put my mind at ease as he led me across that vacant place I did not know. Nothing before and nothing since has brought me such a sense of quiet, such a resonating sense of peace. We rode through much of each day and we rested quietly at night. A campfire each evening cooked our lentils and rice. In the morning I awoke to the fragrant smell of sweet cardamom tea with fresh camel milk. And Americans think Starbucks invented *chai*. Life was simple. Life was sweet. If only that serenity could last.

The days went on and I chose to go north to white-water raft with the son of a friend of a friend. Raised in privilege, *Shaukut* was a *Sikh* by faith, a man of leisure by birth, and an outfitter by adopted trade. At roughly thirty years old, he was, it also turned out, unreliable, pompous, and somewhat reminiscent of an adolescent brat. Promises, outfitter's fees, and deposits aside, nothing he had guaranteed was in fact prepared and it very quickly became my own private *Trip from Hell*. Only now do I look back in perspective and laugh.

The camp's cook and I headed up to camp in a crowded and run-down public bus. In a world of commotion and noise, *Ashok* the cook was a quiet and serious young man with black hair, jet eyes, and a bronze and well-defined face. The ride north to *Rishikesh* was several hours of bad driving, frustration, and disgust as passengers vomited in the aisle, the bus broke down, and a tire went flat. Upon arriving late in the last town, *Ashok* announced that he actually had no provisions, nor any money to buy any food. I had been required to pay *Shaukut* a deposit just so the kitchen would be well-stocked and *Ashok* would be well-prepared. *Shaukut* had given him neither instructions nor cash. Alarm bells slowly dinged in the back of my head.

We quickly bought what we needed and caught a late lunch at a local café. Then we searched for a taxi to carry us the rest of the way to the river camp. Around the mountains in the falling dark, we swerved and wound to the unmarked entrance of the river camp. How *Shaukut* thought I would find it on my own, as he had first suggested, I will never understand. In stark contrast to his helpers, *Shaukut* was a thoughtless and irresponsible man. Only by luck had I learned the day before that the cook was traveling to camp the same day as me. Not above socializing with the help, I insisted we ride together. It was a fortunate, inspired twist of fate for which I will forever say thanks.

Ashok commanded the driver to stop and we exited the taxi in cold, pelting rain. Down the darkened hill through grease-slick mud and silhouetted trees I followed *Ashok* deep into the black of that northern India night. When finally we reached the campsite, there was no one there.

The tent was empty. The camp was dark.

In a hazy distance my alarm bells chimed once again.

Ashok and I sat down in the only tent, a large beige canvas affair set up for the staff. There in the dark and the pouring rain, we wondered if anyone else would come. To pass the time we discussed life, liberty, *Shaukut*, and the challenges of our trip. The rain fell in heavy sheets as the minutes and hours slowly ticked by. When at last one helper arrived, I learned the full, sad state of affairs.

Despite *Shaukut's* repeated assurances to me in *Delhi*, not a thing was prepared. My arrival was, in fact, a complete surprise to his staff. No guest tent had been set up, no food had been bought, no river guide had been booked when there were supposed to have been two.

The helper tried to assure me not to worry. He would prepare a fire (*with wet wood in the pouring rain?* Even as a nine-year old Brownie Scout I had learned you cannot do that). He would cook our food (*that I had now paid for twice*). He would pitch a second, more luxurious tent (*this late at night, in this blinding darkness and pouring rain, he would find it where?*). He would get one river guide, he nervously explained before the era of cell phones, but as I was alone, there were supposed to have been two. All would be well, he tried to convince me. But I was weary, and I was now wary. Oh so weary and by now, very wary. Life was no longer so good.

It would all be fine, the helper continually said.

No need to worry, he repeatedly claimed.

Like a broken record, those too-familiar alarm bells now rang loudly, again, and again, and again.

Tired, wet, cold, hungry, and mad, I finally blew my stack. *Don't shoot the messenger*, they say, but in this pitch-dark, rain-soaked and lonely

Indian night I came frightfully close. I skipped dinner to the men's great dismay. I was far too tired and frustrated to eat.

I am, if nothing though, a determined survivor and eventually my senses took over; I began to develop a plan. I laid claim to the one standing tent, though in the absence of a second, I said those men I didn't know could sleep there in the tent with me, too. I canceled my much-anticipated raft trip that was to have been the next day. I bedded down on a wobbly cot in the uncomfortable cold and the unwelcome dark. I slept fitfully through the night, awakening periodically to hear the heavy rain and the river's ominous roar. Visions of deadly flash floods sweeping campers away to a violent and watery death ran circles and skipped and jumped repeatedly through my mind. I wondered just how close the river flowed, as I had arrived in the dark and hiked directly down a steep path into the woods. With only a dim flashlight to brighten the darkened way, I had seen no sign of the river, but now in the black shadows and the echoing cold I heard its angry roar. I prayed to no one in particular, as I lay awake that night. *Would fate please guide me in safety through the night, and awaken me in the morning in a tent that had held its place on the rain-soaked ground.* At that late hour, in the mountains, in the remoteness and dark of the lonely Indian night, there was little else I could do.

At the much-welcomed break of an early dawn the sound of eager voices dragged me unwillingly from my fractured and troubled sleep. The rain had stopped. The ground was saturated but the tent still stood. As the sun rose, I learned the river was not as close as I had once feared and I silently thanked the gods of fate, whoever and wherever they may be. The guide was energized and ready to start, but I was very ill at ease. Images of me in an out-of-control raft on a violent and angry flood-choked river played very strongly in my mind. I stayed resolute in my decision to cancel the white-water rafting trip. The staff tried unsuccessfully but hard to get me to change my mind. Concerned about the lack of preparation coupled with the force of the rain and the sound of the river the night before, I stood firm. No amount of pleading convinced me to change my decision and raft down a swollen flood of raging water with half the necessary crew.

"It will be a problem to get back down to the nearest town," they offered.

My thoughts stopped cold in their tracks.

No buses passed this way, it seemed, and the occasional taxi was very exceedingly rare.

How did they leave the camp? I probed in curiosity and new concern.

"We ride the transport trucks," was their response.

There was a heavy, pregnant pause. The uneasy reality of my predicament on the rain-soaked side of that distant mountain began to rise with the morning sun.

"You *hitchhike?*" I asked, ever hopeful the response would be a stalwart '*no.*'

"Yes," they confirmed.

My hope sank hard like a lead balloon.

"That is, if the drivers will take us; often they won't."

In the emotionally-loaded distance between the river and the road, I recalled with a chill in my bones, the opening scene of a French novel I had just recently read. A couple of twenty-something year-old backpackers hitchhiked north in this same region, accepting a ride on a local transport truck. The driver was a slithery type with a dark and calculated agenda of his own. He savagely raped, robbed, and murdered the girl and took her boyfriend for a nasty ride before dumping him just a bit further down a mountain road not so different from my own. It was just a story, *but not so extraordinary in this place,* some Indian acquaintances I spoke with in *Delhi* had said.

The sun was dazzling and the sky was clear in a picture book sort of way. But there was a thick tension hanging in the air. As I reviewed my options, my choice became clear. Just as I had commandeered the tent the night before, I commandeered *Ashok,* the cook, that early uncomfortable March day. *He would go with me to flag down a truck,* I explained confidently, leaving no room for debate. And then he would ride *with* me into town. Once I had secured a taxi-for-hire to return me to *Delhi*, he would be free to go his own way. I don't think they believed me at first, a foreign woman so assertively directing traditional Indian men. But I stood firm, they eventually gave in, and we continued on my way, hitching a ride on the first transport truck that came by.

The horns screamed, the beggars called, the touts aggressively cried out. The noise and chaos and fumes that just weeks before had been an ever-present annoyance were now a welcome scene. Back in *Delhi* from my exasperating excursion up north, I rode the rickshaws, had my horoscope read, my muscles rubbed, my shoulders massaged. I toured. I shopped. I ate. And I slept. In the peace and safety of a quiet hotel that was far from a threatening river's bank. After the nightmare in the mountains, it was heaven to be once again on familiar, if chaotic, ground.

But comfortable as the familiar was, I was born a gypsy. The road eventually beckoned me once again like a resonating, primal call. And like any good pilgrim, I followed the song in my heart, my blood, my genes, and my feet. I decided to travel northeast, to *Bodghaya*, where a twist of irony has visited an aggressive culture of violent crime on the region where *Buddha* found compassion, enlightenment, and peace. Annabel had just joined me from Tajikistan for a wonderful reunion of sorts. We bought rail tickets and ventured forth.

All started well. We were in a private compartment in the *Ladies' Car* on the overnight train, a dreary four-berth cabin with two over-stuffed, dark green vinyl-covered bunks on each side, a grimy window, and an uncooperative sliding door. We chatted, we reminisced on our shared days in *Dushanbe*. We exchanged tales of our respective ventures in India. We laughed, we commiserated, and we talked. As night approached we locked the door and climbed on our berths to sleep.

What are all these men doing here? I wondered silently in alarm as I opened my eyes, the scene before me came into laser focus, and I remembered where I was. Just a few hours before, four of us had been alone in our *private* compartment of the ladies' car of the train, accompanied only by each other and the rhythmic sound of the train beating its tracks. Two Japanese girls, Annabel, and me. We had carefully locked the compartment door as we rolled forth through the consuming dark. We had closed our eyes to sleep, at ease in each others' company, with the lock on the door in this segregated car of the train. But now, as I awoke in the middle of the night, shadows of more than a dozen sultry, dark-eyed Indian men came sharply into view. I looked about quickly to take full count of the scene.

What happened to our private ladies' car? We four were no longer alone in the depth of the night as this train rolled forward into the blackened Indian abyss.

Annabel was fine, alone on her berth. I was all right on my bunk. Where the Japanese girls had once stretched out on the opposing berths, I now saw two tight, round balls with arms wrapped around bended knees, cowered heads, and fearful eyes peering at the several figures well-entrenched on their beds. There were also a dozen more men crowding the very narrow six-foot stretch of floor. I had had no problems traveling alone on the night trains in *Rajasthan*, but India's Northeast is a rough-and-tumble place.

The odds of this turning out well were not in our favor, and the price for four foreign women late at night was potentially very, very high. Annabel, me, two Japanese girls. And a car full of Indian men subscribing to the notion that possession is nine-tenths of the law. We four had all paid well for private space in this women-only *ladies car* that was in theory supposed to be safer, more private, quieter, more secure. Concerned about our safety late at night, I was unwilling to share our space with these unsavory, guiltless men looking for a free and comfortable ride. Sharp, penetrating stares met me as I flipped on the light and sat up on my bed.

"Please leave," I said firmly.

But the men did not move.

"Good-bye."

"Leave. Get out." I pointed sharply at the door.

The men did not budge. Not one moved. Not a centimeter. Not a foot. Not a quarter of an inch.

"Go on, get out. **Get out**."

Annabel joined in my directives, while the two Japanese girls watched frozen in silence and fear, their eyes wide, faces drained, and lips pursed in very thin lines. Despite our directives, our stern commands, the men did not move. Hoping eventually someone would help, we ratcheted up our volume until it approached a near-fever pitch. We built such a commotion the men finally departed, looking very annoyed. Having been so summarily displaced by four women, they no doubt wondered disdainfully what *our* problem was.

"*Madame*," the park guide said with a somewhat impatient edge to his voice.

"If you want a guarantee...... **GO** to the **ZOO**."

It was one week later. The eight-foot crocodile quietly slid past us barely leaving the slightest ripple of a wake. Holding a day-old kill in his jaws, he moved effortlessly through the brackish water with the smooth, fluid motion of an eel. The deer he carried must have been attacked in a violent splash of water and the lightening-quick flash of a jaw, down at the murky water's edge. With no way to chew his dinner, Nature taught this powerful, prehistoric beast to drag his prey around in the water for a couple of days, until its flesh was rotten and its bones were soft so its body could be swallowed whole. In those few moments when the crocodile and its prey slid by, we were witness to a call of the wild and a command of genes that reach back many centuries, long before either I, or that crocodile were born.

In the weeks since I first arrived in India, the temperatures and humidity had soared, giving a paste-like quality to our clothes; they clung hungrily to our skin. We had left *Bodghaya* a week earlier and gone on to *Ranthambore* Park. I had not thought I was asking for much, just an assessment of the odds that I might see one of India's wild tigers, one of the world's finest cats. In all fairness, this poorly-paid guide probably suffers my same, tedious question innumerable times each day from the many other tourists who visit this park, all with the same common goal. *Ranthambore*. It is India's home to one of the country's largest remaining populations of tigers in the wild. Proud, quiet, cunning animals of rich, earthen copper and lustrous jet black. Big cats that move with precision and purpose and stealth. Elusive animals. I took hopeful Jeep rides at dusk and at dawn. Four times in two days. We saw crocodiles. We saw iridescently-colored peacocks. We saw pythons in the brush, and we saw monkeys, and rodents, and small deer. But the tigers, the whole purpose of our trip? More than once on our game drives we stopped. And waited. And waited. And watched.

"*He's in there,*" whispered the guide, in hushed words that held the seductive promise of a gambler's lucky win.

We watched the grass like hawks, looking for the slightest twitch, the faintest parting of two parallel blades. We listened for the warning calls of the surveillance birds. For the flight, in alarm, of miniature deer. We listened for the low, earthly growl of a hungry tiger. But the air was quiet. The tall grass was perfectly still. More like a silent photo capturing a snapshot in time than real life where the grasses bend and sway as a wind blows lightly or a bird alights.

We watched. And we waited. And we watched.

"*I'm sure he's there,*" the guide shared with us in an encouraging, conspiratorial tone.

And we waited, we waited, we watched. The birds took flight. A small butterfly with lemon chiffon wings passed on a whisper through the openness of our Jeep. *He must be there*, said the guide. *I'm sure.* The sun was setting and the park was about to close.

Heightened expectations................dashed hopes. To our great disappointment at not sighting a tiger, the day was ending; it was time to leave. As I continued back to *Delhi* the following morning, Annabel returned on another game drive. They found a pair of tigers mating in clear view. For me, however, it was, **Madame, go back to the zoo**.

Over more than two months India offered me colorful, unexpected adventures and numerous stories to tell. In my days, weeks, months of crisscrossing the South Asian subcontinent. India, too, had become my teacher, my educator, my school. In this populous nation of varied landscapes, languages, cultures, and cuisines, I had found what I had not sought. I had learned the strongly magnetic and deeply soothing spiritual power of the desert. I learned that nothing speaks to my psyche and my soul like the dry, sun-baked sand. And I was reminded of the extraordinary beauty of the night sky. I learned that nothing soothes my worn body or my weary mind like a star-studded blanket over a quiet bed on the desert dunes. So clear was this lesson, it would eventually lead me to move my home to a different desert at a different time.

I learned in the hills of India's North, the train to *Bodghaya*, and the tigers of *Rhantambore*, that much as I might want to try to control the people, the animals, and the things around me, my sphere of influence is, in fact, quite limited. It is in fact, quite small.

I learned, too, that what a wise and worldly friend once told me is true. *The most important things to take when you travel are a strong stomach and a good sense of humor.* I had carried a strong stomach and it had served me well. Amidst the chilies, the food stalls, the dust, and the dirt over nearly three months, I did not once fall ill. And the humor? Well, from time to time it wore thin. But my friend is right. It cushions the disappointments, lightens the communication, lubricates the problems, and turns the misfortunes into grand adventures. *Do take a strong stomach and a good sense of humor.* They will serve you well.

Eight Hundred Pounds of Muscle and Might

Rwanda (2002)

So Red Riding Hood set off with her basket through the woods.
Many people believed the forest was
a foreboding and dangerous place and never set foot in it.

James Finn Garner, "Little Red Riding Hood,"
Politically Correct Bedtime Stories

He looked at me with an intensity that made my heart stand still. His thick, Herculean arms, his dark, ebony-colored eyes, and his unflinching, hard, black face stood just a few very short feet from mine.

Deep in the thick green jungle of northern Rwanda, we were almost within touching distance; we were nearly face to face. This may have been the land of mountains and mist, but it was also the land of feared and fearless rebels and ruthless poachers heavily armed with deadly firepower and unrepentant greed. Not daring to move, not wanting to break this moment, not wanting to incite a reaction for which I was not well-prepared, I held my breath as eight hundred rock-solid pounds of power and might considered me carefully. They held my fate in their command.

We had traveled one hundred-fifty kilometers to the far Northwest of Rwanda to reach this most extraordinarily beautiful place. Past verdant hills dressed in a thick carpet of lush trees. Between clustered mountains, through fertile valleys, past dormant volcanoes, and villages of mud brick huts. Over smooth black asphalt and uneven vermilion-colored clay. Around massive cones of green velvet and *chenille*. Through the cool, crisp air, the fresh smell of rich, damp earth, and a plentitude of emerald-tinted leaves. *Milles collines*. A thousand hills. Stretching before me was some of the most inspiringly beautiful scenery my eyes have ever seen.

Once at the park, we climbed for more than two hours through thick jungle. We trudged up the mountain and through the brush to the sounds of an ant's march and a mosquito's wings. We climbed over tangled roots. We slogged through slippery mud and brushed away leafy vines. Branches smacked our arms and slapped our faces; wet leaves caressed our cheeks. *François* bush-whacked the thickest growth with hard, muscular arms and a mean machete. Heavy with anticipation, it was a trying, arduous hike.

We were quite an entourage, as gorilla trackers go. We were only three tourists – two Rwandans and me. The only white one in the bunch, I wondered if the gorillas would pick me out of the otherwise very dark crowd. One guide, three trackers, three military guards, four machetes, and three machine guns marched with us through the green foliage, the thick mosquitoes and the cold, damp mist. This, it became clear, was no ordinary romp in the woods. In fact, it was an exceptional experience few foreigners have, as a perfect storm of logistics, limits, prices, fear, and science worked to keep the number of visitors purposefully very low.

My one-hour permit cost me roughly three hundred-fifty U.S. dollars, a considerable sum. It came with no money-back guarantee. My colleague's permit, with proof of his Rwandan citizenship, cost fourteen. In a country where the majority earn far less than one dollar a day and have multiple mouths to feed, even fourteen U.S. dollars is far beyond the reach of most people. Just for the chance to possibly see, in their own habitat, the famed Mountain Gorillas. *The Great Silverbacks*. It is no wonder few Rwandans buy a permit and go. Some foreigners claim discrimination, saying that the price differential is unfair. But in a land where few individuals make even a tiny fraction of what I as a foreigner do in a year, and where the government is trying hard, with few resources, to protect a species in dangerous decline, is differential pricing really so wrong?

"If a gorilla charges us would they shoot?" my Rwandan colleague asked *François*, nervously eyeing the soldiers with their guns. The tension in Henry's voice and the look on his face betrayed his normally easy-going way.

"Only a warning shot into the air," was the guide's quick, sobering, honest, and unequivocal response.

"You won't shoot the gorilla to save my life?" Henry screeched with a flash of panic in his eyes and fear in his newly high-pitched voice. A look of alarm raced across his face.

"No. So do exactly what I say," *François* replied.

There was a notably weighty pause.

It was just like *Simon Says*, the old childhood game my grammar school mates and I used to play. Simon says *take two steps*. That's what you do. He says *stop*. You follow his command. The guide moves forward. So do you. He stops. You stop. He sits. You sit. He stands. You stand. It all seemed pretty elementary to me but twice *François* gave sharp rebukes when Henry went just a few short feet astray.

Mighty animals that they are, these wild gorillas are uncompromisingly, incomprehensibly strong. One miscalculation on my part and they could have turned me into a warm pile of dead flesh. These are not big, soft, lovable things in a stuffed toy store, or exotic entertainment behind the protective barrier of heavy steel bars at the zoo. They are undomesticated animals with a strong sense of self-preservation, and a very determined mind of their own. We, the tourists, were intruding in their habitat; they were not entering ours. That was a reality we should not ignore.

In sad fact though, we were probably in far more danger from the poachers than the apes, as we were entering *their* territory, too. Lawless and opportunistic, poachers are known Africa-wide as shrewdly ruthless men for whom life holds no value – either the gorilla's life, or mine. A friend who once worked in the game parks of central Africa told me that far more than a close encounter with a pride of lions, he feared an unexpected, chance encounter with a poacher and his gun. He said a lion, unless hungry, would likely let him pass. He knew the poacher, on the other hand, would unquestionably shoot him dead on sight with no hesitation, no reason, and not a drop of remorse.

Just a week before, the trackers had found a young gorilla dead by a poacher's gun, bullets delivered to its chest and its hands severed for sale as macabre souvenirs – a couple of ashtrays for individuals with unimaginable greed and a repulsively, grotesquely inverted sense of right and wrong. It is true that some gorillas in the jungle are killed for food but those hunters don't chop the hands and leave the rest to rot. And killing to fill an empty stomach or feed a family or a village is a far cry from wasting a life for a sadistic trophy that will be used to stamp out cigarette butts in some wealthy man's house. It was on account of the poachers that we three ordinary tourists enjoyed our well-armed and vigilant military escort.

The park rules are deliberate and strict. *Stay at least seven meters back* is Rule Number One. *Stay at least twenty feet back.* The regulation is clear. It was not by intent or even neglect that we violated the most important and most sacred gorilla-tracking rule, designed to help keep the animals healthy and the humans safe. We walked in a single line like a mother hen and her chicks. *François,* then me, then the others, into the far corners of a dense jungle where the leaves dance and the clouds weep. Between thin trees and thick vines. Past giant clusters of green that fingered us as we moved under a canopy of branches that reached far above our heads. When finally we came upon the family of apes, they were in the midst of a bamboo thicket so dense we were within *one* meter, not seven, of the animals before even *François,* our very able guide, could see them.

It was *Gahinga,* a little two-year old, we spotted first. He was sitting immediately in front. You could bet good money that his mother's watchful eyes were not far behind. *François* came to such an abrupt halt

74

that I bumped into him, my nose and forehead hitting the back of his head. Electricity ricocheted quickly through the air. When I saw the first patches of thick, black fur, that first shoulder, the first small hand, tingles ran up my spine and my hair curled as it stood on end.

Gahinga stood swiftly and looked at us for a very long moment that froze in time. Then my young cousin, who at two years old was already stronger than me, raised his small fists and began pounding his pumped-up, puffed-up, barrel-shaped chest. Standing and pummeling his jet-black chest as he did, he could have been the star in the Saturday morning television cartoons back home.

And then..... *Gahinga* reached out toward us with hands one-quarter the size of mine. With his crooked fingers he took deliberate hold of *François'* shirt sleeve. Once again, time stood still and the jungle stood silent as we waited to see what *Gahinga* and his watchful mother would do next. With outstretched arms, he tugged a couple of times on *François'* shirt sleeve. Putting us on notice, *Gahinga* began to chatter away. *François* took heed. In one liquid movement, without the slightest audibly discernable sound, he slid down into a crouching position in the brush to diffuse a situation that could have otherwise quickly turned bad. I quietly followed suit; the others copied me. There we sat silent in the thick brush, in one of the most exceptional moments in my years abroad.

Around us in that jungle, all stood still. The insects were silent. The leaves did not flutter. The branches and the vines did not move. But then something even more amazing than the previous few minutes took place. Our guide began to speak. Not in English. Not in French. Not in local dialect that my colleague would have understood. Not in any language whose words I could comprehend, but in a secret and privileged conversation in the young gorilla's own tongue. By divine intervention or simply sheer luck we had *François,* the country's best guide. A friendly and exceptionally knowledgeable man who takes Rwanda's President on his treks, *François* is well-studied and well-experienced in these gorillas' ways.

For several minutes *Gahinga* and *François* carried on in private conversation until *Gahinga* relaxed, his face softened, and he, too, sat down in the brush.

We looked about. Our eyes adjusted to the cluster of foliage and the dim, filtered light. Under scattered patches of broken sunlight, past translucent yellow-green leaves, the full scope of the scene unfolded slowly; gradually it came clear. There sat mom observantly, to *Gahinga's* right. She was a stout female with fat cheeks, dark, attentive eyes, a big belly, and wide, thin lips. There was a sibling on *Gahinga's* left. Two adult males were not far behind, but mostly obscured from our view. I do not know how many others in the clan the protective layers of the jungle may have chosen, in silence, to hide in a canvas of camouflage. Alone with the gorillas in the hungry clutch of the thick, green jungle, we were not in Kansas, *Toto*, and this was definitely not the zoo.

After twenty infinite minutes of watching *Gahinga* and his clan, we moved slowly and silently ten feet to the left, around a corner framed by tall rods of jade-colored bamboo. Shafts of sunlight fell through thin spots between the slender shoots intricately woven into a fine canopy of leaves far above our heads. Custard-colored light cast a brightness on small patches and triangles and squares against which deep shadows recessed, making corners and crevices a blackened greenish shade of dark.

It was only moments later that *Ubumwe*, the commanding Big Chief, appeared. Eight hundred imposing pounds of solid muscle and brawn, his hard expression was chiseled in black granite, his mouth firmly set. You could almost see the foliage maneuver to stand straight as he confidently sauntered into full view. There was no doubt whose territory we had entered, whose house we were in. When at last *Ubumwe* reached center stage, just a few feet from where we kneeled together in the brush, he sat down in an old rock star's comfortable slouch. Time stopped. An expansive, expectant silence dominated the air. The bamboo stood motionless. The leaves did not shift. Not even the insects fluttered their wings.

From left to right *Ubumwe* surveyed the scene slowly, deliberately, with purposeful, half-caste eyes. With a strong grip and a gnarled hand, he pulled up a pale stalk of wild celery, took a bite, and began to chew with the satisfaction and patience of an old man chewing tobacco out on the farm. He scratched his dark chin with curved fingers and rounded nails. He inhaled deeply. And he sighed. We sat silent, motionless, and we watched.

Our park permits had not simply bought us a pricey entry to a beautiful, remote patch of geography, they had bought us front row seats to a theatrical performance worthy of a *Tony* award; it was a performance that eclipsed all else. We remained silent, we were consumed in awe.

After protracted moments of commanding a mesmerized audience and owning this spontaneous, improvised stage, *Ubumwe* stood. For a brief, studied minute he paused. Then he ambled a few feet, his, broad, black shoulders forward and his powerful arms low. He stopped in suspended animation. He turned his head slightly and with measured eyes, he looked back. For a sliver of an instant I held my breath as if doing so could preserve that unforgettable split second in time. Then like a slow-motion runway model on cue, *Ubumwe* pirouetted once, jutting his hip just ever so slightly to the side. He pouted with thin lips that covered strong, ivory-colored teeth. He struck a measured, fashion mannequin's pose. Again I held my breath, fearing an exhale would somehow prematurely shatter the scene that had taken shape before my eyes. There was an empty space in the air as the others held their collective breath. Then *Ubumwe* moved again. One step…..two….three….a second pirouette. Stop. Turn. Pause. And then he sauntered out. I could almost hear the dance instructor tapping the floor to keep time. Like the best choreographed catwalk performance of *Paris Fashion Week*, *Ubumwe* gave us a carefully orchestrated show.

The jungle was shadowy and quiet with only thin strands of sunlight slipping through the air. There were no birds' calls. No crunching twigs.

There was barely the audible sound of a rustling leaf. Two days earlier, three hundred-fifty U.S. dollars plus a rented 4 x 4 truck and driver, and guide and tracker fees seemed a recklessly high sum to pay, though for this once-in-a-lifetime chance, I did so anyway. Now I would have gladly paid twice.

Dwarfed among the tall, green bamboo, we each sat motionless in the still air on the silent earth, consumed in our own thoughts. Then in walked Charles, the second in command, *Gorilla Number Two*. My eyes grew wide and I could feel my pulse start to race again as we watched Charles move onto the scene. Knowing very well his position in the clan, he moved just a little quicker than *Ubumwe*, and without the Big Chief's imposing attitude. Charles gazed our way with lowered eyelids and a bored, jaded look. One pirouette, a brief pose, and then he, too, ambled off. What beauty and strength and reserve they showed, these distant cousins of mine.

The road back to *Kigali* was a smooth ride as our small car skimmed over new pavement that snaked around hundreds of seemingly ordinary curves. Each bend, though, had its own story to tell. Disinterested in the idea of gorilla tracking at first, Henry was now overcome with emotion; he was thrilled, amazed, awed by what we had seen. He talked effusively about the morning. He also talked about his country, its history, its people, its resources, its wildlife. And he talked about its war. Henry pointed out the bends in the road where barely a handful of years earlier snipers armed with blinding hatred and powerful guns sat on opposing hills and picked off every driver who dared try to pass by, using angry bullets that traveled nearly the speed of light. We passed hills peopled by betrayal, where enemies had once been friends. We traveled through valleys whose walls would scream and whose dead would cry, if only they could talk. This is a country that has known much sadness; it is a country that has known much pain.

In the tragically far too many stories I heard of yet one more internal conflict, one more massacre, one more civil war, one more neighbor killing neighbor, I questioned in unspoken words what sparks such appalling wars. Only in understanding and resolving the causes can we hope to prevent them from happening anywhere else, to prevent them from happening again.

Far from making judgments or laying blame, I came to wonder reluctantly if maybe we human beings are not really all the same. What separates those who kill from those who do not, to me, seems often really just a shockingly thin thread of circumstance. The culmination of collective anger or injustice coupled in a social crucible with just the right extraordinary frustration or economic disparity or incomprehensible fatigue. This was seven years after the Rwandan genocide that rolled across our television screens. The barbaric carnage few outside Africa paid any notice until Hollywood taught history. In 2005, *Hotel Rwanda*, with its sanitized account of one hero reopened at least partially, for a very brief moment, America's eyes to the horrors of the war.

On the one hand, such cold, calculated brutality seems impossible, unimaginable, unfathomable to me. But I have heard too many first-hand accounts in too many countries where I have traveled or worked to not believe it was true. And in Rwanda, as in three or four other times and places before, I witnessed a frightening spontaneous verbal combustion fueled by some deep-seated, unspoken anger or rage that, in my experience and belief, lies just below the surface across much of the African continent and perhaps only very slightly deeper across the rest of the world. Like the flash point in a chemistry lab, where hot oil suddenly ignites without warning, I saw one Rwandan colleague burst unexpectedly with virulent anger late one otherwise forgettable afternoon. In his unexpected explosion of words, he spewed forth the most vitriolic speech, leaving me dumb-founded, in shock. *What is it that underlies such an explosive temper*, I ask myself, *and what is the catalyst that catapults it out of control?*

We continued back to *Kigali* under a warm afternoon sun that mirrored a new dawn and a bright, fresh day. I sensed in Rwanda a vibrancy and an optimism now that I had not expected to see. Women in gaily printed cottons and men in second-hand Western clothes moved with a confident step and a positive energy through the markets, in the villages, on the streets, through the towns. They were animated and smiling. They invested in businesses and learned new skills. They want good work, safe homes, to send their children to school. Just as most of the rest of us do, they want a bright future, and long-lasting peace.

My days in Rwanda were short but they left an indelible impression. If I learned one thing in this country, it was how small my problems are in the face of so many people around me. I have never in my own land lived in fear that my neighbor would one day turn against me in the flash of a gun or the swath of a machete simply because of the heritage of my genes. I have never lived with the hunger that I would not find my next meal, or the fear that I would return home to find my family strewn like discarded logs across the living room floor. But that has been the reality too many have lived while the rest of us often collectively turn our backs.

When I reflect on Rwanda's genocide my heart gets heavy. When I think of those brief but exceptional hours in the jungle I shiver at the toll the civil wars in Rwanda and its neighbors took on the people, and on a broader humanity that includes Rwanda's animals as well. Like Red Riding Hood with her basket, I went into a jungle *many believed was a foreboding and dangerous place.* But while I found danger, I did not find harm. Instead, I found an experience most incredible, an experience most superb. Looking through the bamboo at those gorillas in the mist gave me a new appreciation for the importance of protecting endangered species, something no city zoo ever could have taught. And it was like glimpsing through a window at a metaphor for Rwanda's past. Something that it lost sight of once – beauty, majesty, and strength. And finally, it was like peering at the fragile future Rwandans must work very hard to protect.

I was sad to leave. But just as something primal beckoned and called to *Ubumwe,* leading the Big Chief to exit his stage, my passport summoned me. I said my good-byes. I went to the airport. And I caught yet another plane.

I Was a Very Cheap Date

Morocco (1993 – 1999)

I'm sorry to say, but sadly it's true
that Bang-ups and Hang-ups can happen to you.

Doctor Seuss, *Oh, the Places You'll Go!*

Greg shook my arm gently and woke me up.
"Margaret, it's time to go."
Reluctantly I pulled out of my deep, sleepy fog, only to feel very embarrassed, to feel socially very inept. Greg, a friendly Australian I had only just recently met, had invited me to a charmingly romantic little restaurant for dinner; for my part, I had just *slept* through the meal.

We had met just five days before, at the bus station in *Marrakech*. Two solo travelers in a foreign land. Little did this kind Australian know at that time that before the close of the week he would curtail his vacation, put his own travel plans on hold, and spend his nights wiping down my burning back. It was *OK*, he had assured me later, with an understanding smile and a teasing laugh. *I was a cheap date.* In spite of the multi-course menu and the flavorful cuisine, I had ordered one tasteless, boiled potato and settled into the comfortably deep floor cushions that were our colorful, hand-woven seats. The next thing I knew, Greg had finished dinner, and after just two bites, I had slept through mine.

How *very,* very dangerously sick I had been. For three agonizingly long days my body was on fire at a blazing one hundred-five degrees while violent, raging dysentery turned my insides out. It was August. I was deep in the *Sahara* Desert, an unforgiving inferno of broiling sun and scorching sand that sucks the moisture right out of your body at race car speed. For three frightening days I had not been able to keep even a sip of water down, nor to keep anything else in.

Admittedly, the route to dysentery was an adventurous one. I had arrived in *Casablanca* alone and had taken a night train south. Five hours traveling to the lullaby of a rail car on its silvery steel tracks. The gentle rocking sent me quickly to sleep as we rolled south into the mysterious black of night.

Marrakech is a favorite place for me. The shadowy *souks* lure me with their mystery and their promises and their wares; the carpet sellers call me with their mint tea and exotic charm. The sweet, pungent smell of spices tickles my nose and teases my palate. The blackened olive oil soap softens my skin though it resembles a translucent slab of used car grease. And the sun brightens my spirit while the desert tugs at the innermost reaches of my soul. I spent wondrous days revisiting the markets, hunting for treasures, feasting on spiced olives, fresh apricots, sweet cherries, and a wide assortment of nuts. I savored the cold, sweet taste of pistachio ice cream. I started each day with the robust warmth of a morning bowl of flavorful *harira* chick pea soup that fills your stomach, nourishes your day, and pleases your tongue.

In *Marrakech* time lost its meaning as I ventured through the streets by day and slept on the roof tops at night. After the heat of the afternoon sun I reveled in the soft, cool evenings where a voile-thin breeze whispered quiet secrets in my ears. Twinkling stars promised me a thousand silent wishes would one day come true.

I spent hours visiting the dark, damp *hammams* where strong, corpulent, big-busted peasant women scrubbed me, rubbed me, took every flake of dry skin off my naked frame before attempting to drown me with buckets of water poured repeatedly over my head. They pointed, they spoke behind raised hands and lowered eyes, and they laughed. *Look at the foreign woman. How skinny and pale she is. A strong wind would blow her away.*

I spent late afternoons among the myriad of shifty-eyed rogues at *Djemaa el Fna.* Come five o'clock, as the sun goes down and the temperature drops, a lively cast of characters moved into place and a circus straight out of Charles Dickens came to life. Within minutes the square filled to a standing-room crowd. Tourists watched from the safety of roof-top cafés. But *I* wandered, mesmerized, through the madness below.

The snake charmers, the magicians, the jugglers, the fruit peddlers, and the food carts jostled for my attention, my money, my time. Dancing cobras moved tall to the sway of their handler's flutes. Musicians worked their drums, their seed-filled gourds, and their tambourines, turning loose a tribal rhythm to march through the air. Juice stands sold the sweet liquid gold of a fresh-squeezed orange. Food carts sold flavored rice, cooked meat, cooked vegetables, hot stew. Fortune tellers read palms, they read cards, they read the future through cowry shells.

"You come from a distant land," she said, having quickly surveyed my pale skin and my European clothes.

"You will soon discover many new things," she proclaimed, a stout woman with a leathered face, thick brows, graying hair, and tattooed hands.

Of course. Please tell me something I don't already know.

There is a mystery and a magic – *black magic* some people I know say – in this city of spices and secrets and coral-colored charm. For me *Marrakech* is the land of *Ali Baba,* of *Aladdin* and his lamp, of childhood storybooks about faraway places, exotic names, and colorful dreams. Of riches and rumors, of lush palm-filled oases, flying carpets, shooting stars, caravans, cobras, and whispered intrigue.

Mohammed was an animated thirty-year old *Marrakech* man with the charm of a suitor, the gracious hospitality of an Arab, and the tenacity of a used-car salesman.

"Come look. *Pour la plaisir des yeux. Just for the pleasure of your eyes.* Sit. Let me offer you tea. No need to buy. Please. Just look."

Yeah, I thought sarcastically to myself. I had heard *that* before. *Just for the pleasure of your eyes.*

Well I did not buy anything, but I did sit and look. Over the course of several years I passed many happy hours in *Mohammed's* second-floor shop. Watching carpets carefully unfold like the much-anticipated guide to riches of a well-guarded treasure map. There were solid-colored flat weaves from the South, with tiny geometric patterns etched in contrast across their surfaces, the embroidered woolen traces of a bird's feet. There were charcoal and ivory woolen *hanbels* with patterned stripes, resembling an artist's interpretive rendering of a zebra's back. The shaggy loose yarn on the underside keeps a tired shepherd warm at night as he wraps his shoulders against the cold chill of a biting winter wind. There were thick, soft pile rugs of bold color and hand-tied knots. Mustard, ochre, and blue danced across canvas after canvas until half the room had been unrolled.

I sipped miniature cups of sweet mint tea prepared over the glowing embers of a small charcoal brazier, as I observed with quiet amusement this master of trade courting the tourists who came into the carpet shop after me. Watching *Mohammed* hold court in his shop was the best free entertainment a Moroccan afternoon could buy.

Most tourists I observed flipped through those rugs with impatience and speed, looking for a cheap price on a good piece that perfectly matched their household décor back home. A man or a woman on a mission, too single-mindedly focused on a destination to enjoy the journey along the way. In their consumer-driven haste they do not know what an extraordinary experience they miss. Aside from what the peddlers say, each hand-made carpet tells a rich story to those who will stroke its pile with a light touch and an open ear. If you look closely into the shadowy depths of the yarn, you can almost see the mountains and fields grazed by the animals who gave their wool and the villagers who tend their herds. It is a story of poverty and wealth, not always measured in cash.

If you listen carefully you will hear it whisper the frustration and hopes of the sturdy man who sheared the sheep, and the thin, curly-haired one who dyed the woolen yarn.

As you knead a carpet's body, its beauty, its mass, you can feel the strong, nimble fingers of the humble women who tied the knots, with their colorful headscarves, round cheeks, and warm eyes. With each knot they tie, these women paint a story of their hardships, their sorrows, their families, and their joys in the time-honored patterns of a traditional hand-crafted rug.

If you watch the eyes of the merchant as he unrolls each piece, you can see the character, imagination, and mischief of the sellers who embellish each colorful masterpiece and its roots. If you listen closely, you can hear the rush of the wind, and the warm whisper of sun that steals its color; you can feel the footprints of a thousand tourists, and taste the sweet mint tea that a few of them spilled.

No hand-knotted rug is merely an intersection of color and yarn.

Instead, it is one complicated story of Morocco, woven of poverty and riches, hard work, alluring beauty, marketing, and mystery. It is a tapestry of mountain slopes, walled compounds, veiled lives, of things that are not always what they seem.

"Don't worry," said *Mohammed* frankly as I paused, holding back from stepping on the carpet he had laid masterfully on the floor.

"Walk on it."

"A few stains and a little dirt will increase the value; they make it look old. Don't worry if you spill some tea. I'll just hang it in the sun to dry."

As we left *Marrakech* in the comfort of a modern, well-maintained bus, the High Atlas Mountains unfolded before my eyes. They rose before and around me in rugged splendor and variegated shades of tan and sage and olive and brown. Peasants selling fossilized rocks and agate in beige, rose, khaki, and coffee lined our route as we ascended toward a cloudless, blue sky. We passed simple houses of light-colored stone and cement and the occasional herd of gray-white sheep and goats. The road narrowed and the curves turned sharp with each additional few feet we climbed.

"Do you think my health insurance will cover me if we go over the edge?" asked a young American man seated next to me in the bus as we rounded a particularly sharp mountain bend.

His tanned knuckles were white and his face was drained of blood. He peered down anxiously at the valley below.

"No need to worry," I said confidently. "Just enjoy the view."

If we go over the edge, your concerns will be over, my friend. And it will be life insurance, not a health policy, your family will hope you have. I kindly kept those thoughts to myself.

I was unusually tired the first day after we arrived in *Ouarzazate*, a dusty oasis town. Exhaustion overwhelmed my body and sapped my normally strong, determined will. I wandered aimlessly through the dusty, sleepy streets for less than an hour, then returned, drained, to our charming little oasis hotel. Giving in to a now-crushing fatigue, I resigned myself to a rare afternoon nap, dragging my body and my mattress outside to rest in the shade.

It was just moments after I lay down that my temperature soared from about ninety-eight degrees to a blazing *one hundred and five*. In the thirsty August heat of the *Sahara* Desert, my latest adventure had just begun.

Every day in the developing world thousands of children, women, and men die from diarrheal illness and the severe dehydration it can bring in mere hours. When I became so very feverish and so extremely sick, the camels, the carpets, the beauty, and the romance of this country I love lost all importance. In my tired mind, they were replaced by one, and only one, very real, very serious, very pressing concern. Retaining those precious, life-preserving drops of moisture that in the desert are the most important, most vital key to life. Of the numerous times overseas that I have been wretchedly ill, only once – this time – was I also afraid. Never before, and hopefully never again, had I been so dangerously and so frighteningly sick in such a remote and distant place.

Greg and I had crossed the mountains and ventured well into the desert before I had so unexpectedly fallen so very, very violently ill.

The unabated, gut-wrenching dysentery I developed, coupled with the vomiting, the perilously high fever, and the fearsomely dry, desiccating, infernal *Sahara* heat, threatened ominously to rob me of whatever long and passionate life might otherwise lie ahead. In that dry, baking oven in August, the tepid water of an oasis swimming pool by day and the wet towels Greg used to repeatedly wipe me down in an attempt to cool me off at night unquestionably saved my life. Once more in my travels I saw the kindness of a stranger in a time of need. I have a debt to Greg that will not be easy to repay.

When after four or five days I finally regained my health and my strength, I again saw the beauty and mystique that is Morocco, a country that over the years I have grown to love. If I were an artist, I would move to this land. It is a rugged, magical place that is at once modern and medieval. It is a place that has one foot in the bright future and one in the very distant and colorful past. A place that speaks to me, that sings to me, that warms me and soothes me and feeds my passions and my dreams with its colors, its flavors, and its mystery. Its flower-filled courtyards and its carefully arched doors speak to me of sweet fragrance, blushed cheeks, warm hospitality, and hidden romance. Its gentle corals, salmon, and rose its shades of khaki, sage, olive, gold, and brown color my imagination with mystery and allure. Its ice-cool blue speaks of measured restraint and quiet reserve. And its deep, rich, hunter green speaks of rich forests and cedar-scented hills. Its walled cities and its mountain roads. Its rocks and dunes, its clear skies, succulent fruit, and exotic spice talk to me of flavors and legends and secrets, and nature, and surprise. The crisp lines of blue and white tiles showcase deliberate order and attentive care. The elegant curves of Arabic script demonstrate grace and wisdom and strength. Moth-eaten camels and donkeys. Warm carpets. Cool nights. *Morocco*. It is a montage that feeds my creativity and soothes my soul. It is a place where I am at peace even amid its noise, its chaos, and its dust.

A year earlier I had crossed the same mountains in another quest for romanticized adventures in the sand. I traveled past small villages, houses built of stone and wood and mud. I passed peasants in traditional garb, men in rudimentary straw hats selling fossils, and dusty mules hauling heavy loads. I traveled under clear skies and bleaching sun. Past mammoth piles of gray striped earth heaved upwards unevenly in khaki layers by restless spirits inhabiting the boiling interior of the world below. Thick layers of variegated rock lay crumpled like the tousled blankets of an early-morning bed.

Like so many other foreign tourists before and after me, I had sought my day on the dunes. I chased a beautiful sunrise and a vibrant sunset over the waves of a thousand decades of golden sand. With two French women I met at my hotel, I had followed telephone poles at dawn across the cracked and broken earth toward a distant line at what seemed the end of the earth. In a well-worn, rented car we traced a barely discernable desert track as far as the eye could see. Three women in search of the dunes, we were accompanied only by the still air and the crunching sound of gravel beneath the tires of our weary, slate-blue car. With curiosity, bravado, and nerve, we rumbled and bounced into a fabled place where camel caravans set out for *Timbuktu* and the rest of Africa, many miles and one and a half months to the south.

It was a great leap of faith to follow those tall, straight poles. *Were we on a bold path to the dunes, or a dusty trail to our death?* If the latter, we would not be the first adventurers to meet our demise in the clench of the dry *Sahara* sand. One after another, those faded brown-gray sentries called us forward, fifty rugged meters at a time.

The dunes beyond *Zagora* were magic; they offered the whisper of a promise in a seductive lover's dream. A gentle warm orange greeted us as the sun began to rise. Shining gold followed, then the bleached-white color of sun-baked glass. As we parked our car at the little *auberge* and climbed the dunes on foot, the shifting sands of a million years worked our muscles even as they gave way beneath our weight. *What is it about the desert that so quiets my mind and pulls at my heart and my soul?* The air was parched. My lips were dry. My voice was hoarse. But my spirit was at peace.

What power those quiet dunes hold. Able to hide a secret or lay bare a crime with the mere whistle of the wind, these dunes control the fate of every man and woman who ventures into their midst. They are able to bring life to an unexpectedly abrupt halt in the desert's infinite expanse and bone-dry air, able to turn bright colors bleached-white under an unforgiving sun or to blacken the mid-day air with the blinding darkness of a thick curtain of sand in the open sky. What history these dunes keep silently to themselves. Ancient tales of salt and gold, of slaves and silver and silk. Of penetrating black eyes. And turbans wound tight. *Let me identify you before you recognize me.* Of sabers and camels and swords. Of star-guided caravans and beautiful moonlit nights.

We were out standing tall on the dunes when the distant early afternoon sky grew black and a once feather-light breeze grew strong. Within minutes grit blew with the wind, scratching our eyes and grinding sharply against our skin and our teeth. At that moment it was no surprise that the sand in a lifetime of bread in the desert measurably wears down a nomad's bite. As the darkness moved closer like a thick, rapidly encroaching fog, we beat a hasty retreat to the shelter of the little *auberge*. A threatening sandstorm was in its approach. These storms may last an hour or they may settle in for a week. Ours, in two hours, was gone. The gods had teased us but this time they did not torment.

As we awaited our dinner of *couscous* and stew, the dining room at the *auberge* began to fill. One and two at a time, tall, dark-skinned men strolled in. Their long, flowing cotton caftans of soft periwinkle blue and big knives in intricately tooled leather sheaths spoke of mystery and intrigue. Blue gauze wrapped methodically around their heads like an elegantly coiled snake revealed only cunningly observant eyes of rich black coal. A mixture of Arabic and *Tomachek* words filled large pockets of the still, evening air, expanding to cover any void. We three foreigners exchanged uneasy glances as hand-rolled cigarettes were lit and the burning smell of marijuana began to permeate the room. The prospect of doing time in a Moroccan jail did not fit the French women's travel plans. Nor did it fit mine.

We finished our meal, we paid our bill, and we retired to the privacy of our shared room. There I quickly fell into a deep sleep in a lumpy bed, feeling relatively safe in the knowledge that for once in my far-flung and adventurous travels I was not alone.

In the morning we awoke to the disproportionately loud blare of a small alarm clock in a chilled and vacuous room. *Was it really time to get up? Did we have to get out of bed?* We bundled up and trundled out into the cold desert air as a fine, yellow-white line at the edge of the sand turned pink, then orange, then lustrous gold. It was the gracious gift of another Moroccan sunrise. In a matter of moments a bright yellow flooded the sky. With great splendor, the sun climbed upwards, filling the day with light and signaling that it was time for us to go. We fueled our departure with strong coffee, freshly baked bread, and dates at the *auberge*. It was time to leave. With an unexpected feeling of sadness, we climbed into the car and followed those telephone poles two and a half hours back to town. Fortunately for us, cell phones had not yet arrived.

Morocco keeps calling me back and in yet another year on another trip I continued farther south, crossing over the breathtakingly beautiful *Tiz'n'Tes* mountain pass. In a "shared" taxi that I had hired alone, I traveled to the walled city and veiled women of *Taroudant*. It was there I first tasted the ripe fruit of the Prickly Pear cactus, offered by a friendly old man with a tattered straw hat, a grizzled jaw, and several missing teeth. He stood in the market with an old scarred and stained plastic bucket of the succulent, red, egg-shaped fruit. He stood next to the bronze-skinned man who sold inexpensive, hand-made sandals cut from recycled pieces of used rubber tire tread. They were next to the vendors wearing makeshift newspaper sailboat hats against the burning sun, as they sold large sacks of imported white rice. It was also there in the brilliant heat of the North African summer day, that I met the *Shoe Shine Mafia* of *Taroudant*.

Young *Ahmed* approached me politely and tentatively enough. Slim and sandaled, with narrow shoulders, ragged, navy-colored pants, and a dusty chocolate brown shirt, he looked about nine or ten years old. His hair was curly and short. His palms were stained with dark shoe wax. His fingernails were ringed with black.

"*Cirer les chaussures, Madame?*" Shine your shoes?

His tools were ready and his eyes held hope. I looked down with embarrassment at my dust-covered black leather hiking boots. I could not, in good conscience, turn him down.

With my easy approval, *Ahmed* went ambitiously to work. He dusted, he polished, he buffed, and he shined. After several minutes of elbow grease my well-worn boots looked remarkably new; *Ahmed* had earned his pay. We had agreed ahead of time on an acceptable price, and I paid *Ahmed* the *dirhams* he was due. He thanked me quietly and turned to walk away. It was then I saw the cold realities of one more slice of Moroccan life.

No sooner had I paid young *Ahmed* and he had turned to leave, but an older boy arrived. A puffed-up, broad-shouldered, testosterone-filled adolescent thirteen or fourteen years old. He barked a few sharp words and *WHACK!* He smacked *Ahmed* hard on the side of the head. There was a reluctant touch of hands. *Ahmed* turned back. His eyes had lost their sparkle, his head was lowered, his chin tipped down, and his earlier smile had disappeared. The shoe shine mafia had just called in their take, and from *Ahmed's* demeanor, I believe it was no small sum.

Venez avec moi. "Let's go for a walk," I said quietly, when the two of us were once again alone.

We rounded a corner and walked down the block, out of sight. We talked for a few minutes. I shook his hand. The sparkle came back to his young eyes.

It was mid-summer when the solar eclipse was scheduled to occur. Across the North African *Maghreb*, governments declared a national holiday, closed offices, closed schools. Businesses shuttered their windows and closed their doors. Taxis and buses stayed parked in their *gares.* The government-broadcast warnings against looking directly at the sun took on a life of their own. *Don't look at the sun* became......*Don't go outside*.....which became *Don't let the light into your house, your office, your store. Put on your sunglasses. Wear them, even indoors, with the shutters closed and the curtains drawn. And don't leave the animals outside.*

I heard more than one first-hand account of families who brought the barnyard into the house. *Into the living room.* The chickens. The goats. The sheep. Right inside with dad, mom, and the kids. Perhaps they thought if touched by the sun, the animals would not only go blind but would also go sterile or mad. Like the old game of *Chinese telephone*, the further it traveled, the wider and the wilder the government's warning to avoid looking directly at the sun grew.

The eclipse quietly came and silently went. With a collective sigh of relief, the population relaxed, opened the windows, opened the doors, took off the dark glasses, and let the animals back outside. With few, if any, ill results the much-talked about phantom danger had passed. Some Westerners laughed, but we, who have a good understanding of science and easy access to reliable news, too quickly forget the challenges for those who do not.

Days later, after a few dull hours of waiting on a hard seat in a shabby transit station, it was finally time for my bus to depart. I had been spoiled by very good transport in Morocco, but this bus was a beast of a different breed. At least an estimated thirty-some years old, this tin can on wheels needed a good coat of paint, new brakes, better shock absorbers, several uncracked windows, fewer passengers, and a lot more space.

Packed in like flattened sardines from the very start, our condition only grew worse. As we passed the edge of town, the driver stopped. He pulled out small plastic stools and filled the narrow aisle with another twelve passengers. *W'alai!* There was barely room to breathe, but no one said a word. I watched silently as more people and buckets and parcels and bags poured in. We became a composite of elbows, ribs, and knees, parcels, babies, and bags as the dangerously overloaded bus swung recklessly around bends and charged at full speed up the road. This was the route heading north.

When finally we arrived up in the *Rif* Mountains, I unfolded myself and stumbled out of the bus. Things were noticeably different. The air was cool. The trees were green. In the sky there were puffy white clouds the color of fresh-fallen snow. And the buildings and walls and alleyways were blue. A cool, smooth, translucent, white-washed blue that felt like a welcome block of melting ice after the searing heat of the South. This was the famed town of *Chaouen*, of *Chefchaouen*. Known for its marijuana and *hashish* trade, and its beautifully refreshing, translucent ice-blue paint.

Enchanted by the change of architecture, I began to wander about, to relish in solitude the change of scenery, the calming, cool change of color.

But, my relaxing promenade was not meant to be. Repeatedly in Morocco's South I managed to walk endlessly on my own through the streets, the *souks*, the markets, the alleyways, with few disturbances. *Chefchaouen* was a different case. It was a world apart. Barely had I taken ten steps before a determined young man stepped resolutely up to my side. He offered his guide services but I declined. I wanted to explore in solitude. I wanted to wander about unencumbered and alone.

He tried a second approach, saying he would simply accompany me along the way.

Wise to the age-old tour guide game, I said *no thanks, I preferred to walk alone, and that I was not willing to pay a companion or a guide.*

He continued to flank me as I ignored him and walked on ahead.

Did he understand I would not pay him? I stopped and asked, not wanting an unpleasant surprise at the end, for either him, or me.

Undeterred, he continued to follow me as I turned to the left and then meandered to the right, walking through the narrow streets of this beautiful mountain town. For forty-five minutes we carried on this game of make-believe until I was tired of the shadow I had tried unsuccessfully to shake. It was when I returned to my small hotel that he dealt me the much-anticipated blow. *He had guided me through town,* he claimed, *and now I must pay his fee.* I reminded him I had said from the start that I preferred to walk alone and was not going to pay for his guide services or even for him to just follow me about. When clearly he was not willing to take *no* for an answer, I merely turned into my hotel, went up to my room, and left him to fume outside, alone.

What is it about the North in so many countries on earth, that within the singular borders of one nation seems tougher, harder, less friendly, more rigid than the land peopled by its fellow countrymen and women in the South? In all the months I have spent in Morocco's South, not once have I experienced anyone who was anything but friendly, courteous, hospitable, warm. But in *Chefchaouen* in two days I was followed, harassed, sworn at, and verbally abused with harsh thoughts and nasty words. To see the ethereal, ice-blue walls of this artistically unique and visually serene mountain town, though, I would put up with it once again.

Over the course of several years I basked many times for many months in Morocco's sunshine, beauty, culture, and cuisine. My travels there were not without difficult moments. I was insulted a couple of times by strangers. I was followed twice in the streets by shadowy, determined men. Another man grabbed my arm aggressively as I crossed a *Rabat* city street, and I once fell seriously, frighteningly, dangerously ill. Dr. Seuss hit the nail on the head when he said, *Bang-ups and Hang-ups can happen to you.*

In Morocco, if not before, I learned the potholes and the bumps and the cracks in the road will keep coming and I learned to take them in stride; I learned to pick myself up, dust myself off, and enjoy the beauty and adventure that surrounds. Travel is an adventure, a school, a teacher, a gift. It has been my good fortune, that so far in my travels, the bang-ups and hang-ups have been minor and few. They have occurred occasionally and as I continue to travel I will surely face more. When the price climbs too high, I will stop traveling. But so far, for the lessons and the experience and the gifts I have found, the few *bang-ups* and *hang-ups* have been a very small price to pay.

And so, with more voices calling and more places to explore, I once again caught a plane, and I continued on.

The Darkest Hour and the Brightest Sun

Cambodia (2000 – 2003)

How shall I go in peace and without sorrow?
Nay, not without a wound in the spirit
shall I leave this city.

Kahlil Gibran, *The Prophet*

umber 408. Her photo haunts me. Her eyes follow me around the room. I do not know her name but I know her fate. Her being wanders the fields, the rivers, the roads. She is one of the *Lost Souls*, doomed to journey aimlessly through eternity for lack of a proper funeral, for lack of a proper cremation or proper burial, for lack of a proper farewell. She was one of the tragically unlucky ones. Her soft, confused eyes, her full cheeks, and her chin-length dark brown hair carefully documented with a photo, and a large number affixed to her blouse. One of roughly two million Cambodians savagely murdered by the foot soldiers of the brutal *Khmer Rouge*. Terrorized, tortured, starved, or bludgeoned to death to save the price of a cheap bullet. *Number 408.* Recorded like ordinary goods in a stockroom inventory list.

What was her crime? Maybe she had gone to school. Or perhaps her father had. Maybe he wore glasses, a sign that he knew how to read. Or maybe it was just that she was pretty or perhaps she did not have a peasant's sun-tanned skin. Maybe no reason at all. We outsiders say repeatedly that *we will never let it happen again.* Yet over and over again it does. Armenia. The Holocaust. Guatemala. Chile. Bosnia. Cambodia.

Rwanda. Sierra Leone. The Sudan. The list goes on. *We will never let it happen again*, but then we do.

Getting to know Cambodia and its people was a bittersweet path. In repeated visits over several years, its troubled past, its awkward present, and its uncertain future slowly unfolded for me in a sad and tentative sort of way. Like its exquisite hand-woven silk, Cambodia unraveled in my hands one very delicate thread at a time.

"I was fourteen when they came to my house," he said softly, with a sad, thoughtful voice and downcast eyes.

I had known this man for three years before he told me of his terrifyingly close brush with the murderous *Khmer Rouge*.

They pointed a gun at me and told me to come. They took me to a place in the road and they told me to get in line; they were taking me to the killing fields, they said. I got in line and I waited to board the truck that would take me to where they would kill me, that would take me to my death. But when my turn came to get in, they stopped me and told me the truck was full. They said they would come back and get me later, but I was lucky. They never returned.

I felt a lead weight expand to block my throat and fill my chest. *What do you say when someone tells you that?* I asked myself, having been raised in privilege and safety and peace. *What do you say when someone tells you how he stared death in the face but somehow beat the stratospheric odds?* What devil-filled nightmares he must have that go unspoken. What questions and guilt he must feel, wondering why he was spared when so many other family, friends, neighbors were not. And why was he born into that horror, that fate, while I was not? *There, but for the grace of God, go I.* My head was reeling and my stomach went tight as I remembered the mountains of fractured skulls, the piles of bones I had seen, the photos I had viewed, and the stories I had heard of the bloody trail of rampage of the infamously brutal *Khmer Rouge*.

A pot-holed road. A motorcycle ride. Fresh papaya, juicy mangoes. Landmines. Artificial limbs. A child pointing a gun. A gentle ride on a quiet river. A one-year old so thin her skin hung in folds on arms no bigger than my thumb. The weathered temples of *Angkor Wat*. A woman being trafficked. A child being sold. Carved *Buddhas*. Sweet mangosteens. Beautiful, hand-woven silks. *Phalla's* smiling face. This is the complicated collage that is Cambodia for me.

My early days down south were of a somewhat sordid and troubled sort. When I first traveled there, I was told to be off the road by dusk. Things were much better, the *KR* largely gone, surrendered, demobilized, defeated, given up. But there were still those sporadic, unpredictable attacks by the few remaining holdouts that no one could foresee. *Don't take the risk*, I was warned, *of traveling after dark*. I needed no reminder of the three foreign backpackers who just a few years before had been pulled off an ambushed train right in the area I was traversing. The television broadcast a few years back that brought me news of their murders while I, myself, was backpacking in neighboring Viet Nam, was still vivid in the back recesses of my mind. In a very sober moment one afternoon my Cambodian colleagues showed me the cursed and lonely site where the train had been stopped.

The drive south went well. Three hours in a private car under threatening, cloud-darkened skies. Past frayed villages and ragged land. Past the splintered and floorless wooden homes where a deeply traumatized people live. Past Buddhist temples, roadside markets, barefoot kids. Past skulls and crossbones painted in black on white to denote land known to have once been mined, though no map tracks the explosive devices' flood-fueled migration routes from one rainy season to the next. Past motorized carts carrying deeply tanned women and men with soft, dark eyes, woven sarongs on their slender hips, blue and white checkered cotton wraps crossed neatly on their heads. Past ox-drawn carts. Past a silent procession of orange-clad monks. A few potholes here and a few more there, but as roads go in Cambodia, this one was good.

The town looked weary, and the people looked oddly aloof as they went mechanically through the daily machinations of life. The plastered buildings with their balconies and columns, high ceilings, and big rooms were the worn and mildewed vestiges of an earlier French colonial time. The driver had dropped me off at a two-story, six-room hotel, opposite the river's edge. It was the only one in town, I was told, that did not double as a brothel and a karaoke bar. I would sleep there, where the late afternoon sun turned a flaming pink before lighting the river on fire. There the outdoor restaurant served stir-fry and beer and the mosquitoes grew fat at night.

My room overlooking the river was clean and tidy and large. A slowly rotating ceiling fan labored to move the hot, heavy, moisture-laden air. On the surface the room seemed pleasant enough, but I would too soon learn of the stories its pale green walls and white, freshly retiled floor could tell. A *Khmer Rouge* interrogation center not so long before, I knew I slept at night with the remnants of the devil and the tortured ghosts of this guest house's hauntingly sinister past.

Over countless days spanning many weeks, I watched Cambodia's stone-carvers making souvenirs for the fledgling tourist trade. I watched hand-weavers working their artisanal, hand-hewn looms. I visited farms and businesses and schools. I met auto mechanics, radio repair men, aid workers, and entrepreneurs. I went to the markets and I walked the streets. I visited the local hospital, with an acquaintance on a mission to check on his friend. Worried more about landmines that maim than nature that can kill, the man had been bitten by a poisonous snake in a field he tilled. When the traditional cures failed, my acquaintance had taken his friend to town. There in a dirty provincial hospital bed he had laid suffering, trying desperately to hold on to a fragile life. But there was no anti-venom to counteract the poison coursing relentlessly through his veins; by the time we arrived the next morning, all we found was an empty room. The worn, discolored mattress he had been on just the day before now lay unused. I knew without a word that he had not made it through the night. In the wake, he left behind a young wife and seven young kids. This is a land of depressingly ruinous odds. Whom the KR did not kill, the landmines have not maimed, the dysentery,

Dengue Fever, or malaria have let live, the traffic accidents or the venomous snakes too often take as theirs.

Over time, I spent weeks in a tiny village up north close to the Thai border. It required a torturous all-day ride over nearly impassable roads, the worst I have ever seen. In four-wheel drive we bumped and rolled and twisted and turned, over thick mounds, around deep craters, through slick mud, shifting sand, and thick clouds of beige-colored dust. I held on tight to the roll bar for more than eight hours and kept my head tucked low. It was a grueling ride but time in the remote village was my just reward. There among newly trained hand-weavers I saw enormous pride and a strong determination to get beyond the all-too-recent and devastatingly cruel past. Men and women, young and old, were patching bodies and healing spirits through the craft and majesty of Cambodia's exquisite silk. Mostly the survivors of detonated landmines, these people overcame great hardship, adversity, and pain to build a new life on renewed hope and lustrous thread. Ivory, gold, blue, violet, fuchsia, turquoise, kelly green. The colors of aspirations and dreams, of tears and devastation and strength, of a sorrowful past and a brighter future. These are not the historical colors of traditional Cambodian silk, but rather they are the modern colors of a fresh new day.

Even those traumatized by the horrors of this country's recent past speak with optimism of a *new Cambodia,* and they are trying hard to move forward. Not unlike the second-hand tools for sale in the market, these women and men seek a new purpose in life, their core solid, but their edges scarred and chipped and splintered and worn. It is a painstakingly hard road, but landmine survivors are reclaiming their dignity, their bodies, and their lives. Craftspeople are re-embracing their skills. Students are returning to school. On a daunting, frightening, and unfamiliar path, they now and then stumble and fall, intimidated or overwhelmed by the realities of today's world's demands. Their history haunts them even in their guarded hopes and their tentative dreams. The *Khmer Rouge* taught Cambodia that education was the ticket to your execution and ambition was a sentence to death. Facing the enormous psychological challenges of reconciling the opportunities of the future with their experiences in the past, many Cambodians I met progressed to a certain point then unexpectedly backed off, recoiling as if in a renewed fear of the exorbitant price they would have once paid for having an education or wearing glasses or holding a privileged or responsible job. Their collective wounds are slow to heal but one day at a time they are moving on.

It was eight o'clock. The traffic down below was noisy and the mosquitoes serenaded my ears, but the air was sweet, and smooth coconut curry warmed my palate as a glass of cool white wine softened the sharp edges on my day. We conversed on the balcony of a restaurant downtown, my very dear friend Rick and I. From distant lives on another continent and a different time, it was good to see Rick who was far more knowledgeable in this country's ways then I would ever be. We talked long into the night over chili-laden food and ice-filled drinks, in a vain attempt to explain what was happening in the confused and confusing worlds around us. For me it had been a long, hard day. One that started first with tragic news. I learned that morning that two young employees at my favorite *Phnom Penh* hotel had just been hit by a car. One was dead. One was clinging to his life, but perilously close to death. I had not known them well, but I knew them well enough. Over the years I looked forward to their familiar faces each time I returned to *Phnom Penh*, to one of my many homes away from home. Their smiles, their greetings had brightened each day. Now I would not see one alive again, and possibly not the other.

Having heard the news, I went to the hospital. Asking questions in English and French, and wandering the stagnant halls for an hour, I finally located *Samnang*. Lying motionless in a stuffy room on an old metal bed, he wore only boxer shorts with a dirty rag thrown over his forehead. In obvious pain, he opened his sagging eyes just a bit when I spoke; a thin smile emerged on his tired face.

How was he doing? He had broken bones; he was not sure how many. *Two*, he thought the doctor had said. But I saw no cast. His head hurt, but the doctors did not say why. *Was he really getting any medical care, or merely a bed and a bill?* The doctors thought maybe he had an internal abdominal injury, but they were going to send him home. At thirty or forty or fifty dollars a day, and a salary of less than eighty dollars a month, the hospital is expensive and he had barely any money to pay.

What is the cost of a life? In some countries the actuaries and economists will tell you it is many millions of dollars for the elite. In some countries it is mere pennies for the poor. A Cambodian friend once told me that in his country, *only a life* is cheap. *Send him home.* So easy to throw a life away because one cannot afford a few dollars of medical care. Disturbed by that thought, I paid a large part of his hospital bill, sending money through a trusted Cambodian friend to make sure my dollars did not go astray in the hidden corners of the hospital's bureaucracy or the hands of its poorly paid help.

In the dark shadows of these young men's tragedy, I found there was an important lesson for me. How something small, just minutes of my time, can mean the world to others. It was with a heavy heart that I went to the pagoda to pay my respects to *Senath's* family. The funeral was to be the following day, but the daily fee for the obligatory chanting monks must have been prohibitive, because as I arrived at the pagoda in the late afternoon sun, I found in surprise that the funeral had just begun.

Not quite sure what to do, I looked about for some suggestion, some roadmap, some recognizable cultural clue. Finally I saw familiar faces. They motioned me over, and I joined them in the quiet, somber crowd. One acquaintance took my hand and tied a red string around my wrist. Another man handed me an empty envelope for cash, and a small bouquet. *I should add some small money to the envelope and give it with the flowers to the family*, he advised. Giving me the flowers he had brought, he now had none to give himself but he did not want me, as a foreigner, to suffer the embarrassment of empty hands. As the funeral went on, these friends took care to explain the rituals. When it was time to pass the

109

casket, they led me by the hand. When it was time to pay respects, they introduced me to *Senath's* mother and his widow. Bowed heads shaded quiet tears that rolled gently down their cheeks. In one swift moment these two women had lost the one and only source of income and support in their lives. What did the future hold for them now? It was a sad afternoon.

Word traveled fast. When I arrived back at my hotel, celebrity status greeted me as the doorman thanked me for paying my respects. The telephone operator phoned my room to say she appreciated me helping to pay the hospital bill. The housekeeper came to my room and in her broken English she blessed me and bowed. The receptionist called me to say thank you as well. For days this went on. Such a small gesture on my part, I learned how very much it meant to people so easily taken for granted by the rich foreigners at this big luxury hotel.

In Cambodia I also learned that in some places the bravery and conviction to stand up for your beliefs and challenge the established ways can earn you a bullet in the head. I had met with *Chea Vichea* only months before to learn about labor union issues. In the ensuing weeks we had talked numerous times. Then like the blackened clouds of a looming storm, the fractured e-mails from a mutual acquaintance became ominous. *Something very worried is happening,* the message said. Probably out of fear for who might read our messages, this acquaintance never quite said what was at bay and for the same reasons I did not think it wise to ask. I did not, unfortunately, have to wait very long to learn. Something *very worried*, indeed. On a plane to Europe one day not so long after I had read the last e-mail, I nearly choked on my coffee as I saw the cover story of his assassination on the front page of the *International Herald Tribune.* What was it *Phalla* had told me? *In Cambodia only a life is cheap. Chea's* life may have held no value for his foes except as dead, but for *Chea,* the cost of standing up to the labor lords had in fact been very dear.

While this country has its demons, it has its rich cultural heritage as well. If there is anything that embodies the beauty of the best of the *Khmer* past, it is the legacy of its traditional silk. Lustrous, regal, and fluid, its substance and its patterns reflect Cambodia's tradition, art, agriculture, and skill; its icons represent the legendary religion, architecture, and dance. Deep reds, carnelians, and burgundies. Dark green, warm gold. The painstaking *ikat* dyeing technique depicts the ornate temples, the gentle flowers, and the elegantly symbolic *Apsara* dance. Colored waves and diamonds behold the passion, the patience, the strength, and the spirit of a people who have struggled. With a tired sadness the faded glory of Cambodia's beautiful antique silks now hangs for sale in the urban markets, destined for those foreigners who appreciate and can also afford its beauty, while the villagers to whom it once belonged give it up in exchange for a few good meals, or the price of a young pig.

One hour by single-engine Cessna and an overnight in an elegant old world, colonial style hotel transported me from village to life in the colonial times. I had traveled west to visit the famed *Angkor* temples, *Angkor Wat*. Shielding me from the morning sun was a cracked and broken temple, just a darkened shadow of its much-celebrated past. A weathered body of gray stone, its time-worn surface covered with intricately carved *bas-relief* depicting the history and culture of a distant era long gone by. The cool gray stone, now blackened with fine, velvet-like mold, fights today for its very existence. Just like the landmines that steal villagers' legs, illicit artifacts traders break and steal the temples' carvings and behead the *Buddhas*. In this twisted, destructive competition both nature and man have converged, joining hand-in-hand. What the traders do not steal, the torrential monsoon rains work to wear down while python-like roots of native trees wrap entire buildings, entire structures in their stranglehold, preparing to greedily swallow their prey.

I traveled to *Siem Reap* each time on local planes, but today most visitors to *Angkor Wat* take direct flights from Bangkok or *Ho Chi Minh City*. They drop in for a few hours or maybe a few days. They view the temples, miss the people, skip the markets, and spend all the money to pay for their Cambodian vacation outside the country. Paying from home through package tours for this kingdom's treasures, the money for their flights, their hotels, and even their food mostly stays abroad, doing little to help the country they travel so far to see. Such a shame it is that the one big tourist draw this country holds makes mainly those outside its borders rich.

Days later my eyes adjusted to the darkness, my nostrils to the musty smell. My ears tuned in and tuned out the beggars' calls. I was back in *Phnom Penh*. I made one last trip to the market before moving on. It is a fascinating place. A shadowy puzzle of crowded stalls, uneven walkways, dimly lit aisles. It is part *Pandora's Box*, part back alley, part mystery, part garbage bin, part treasure trove. A stockpile of antiques and fabrics, a source of good bargains, hot meals, and cheap clothes. It is also a den of iniquity filled with counterfeit cds and copycat goods. It is a *Mecca* for the beggars, an opportunity for the pickpockets, and a haven for the touts. You can buy batteries, paper plates, plastic flowers, carved stone. There, in the tiny stalls of the inner sanctum of this poorly-lit maze, you can buy a fake *Rolex*, old loom parts, carved *Buddhas*, cheap perfume, old silk. You can drink soda pop, coffee, snake wine, liquor, or tea. You can eat noodles, fried spiders, fresh mangoes, curried vegetables, or rice. It is a fire trap, a tourist destination, a place of intrigue. I passed many happy hours within the market's walls over the course of several years.

Travel is a teacher, and in one stark moment much later, this faraway country with its hardships and its history and its lessons came unexpectedly back to me at home in the United States. One day, amid the cactus and the sunshine of southern Arizona I learned in perspective just how easy my life had been and just how truly spoiled I am. Back in the U.S. I became temporarily distraught and momentarily depressed on learning I needed an infected bone surgically removed. *Amputated.* That cold word sat frozen on the desk between the doctor and me as he reviewed the x-rays and the test results and listed my options one more chilling time. *Give up part of my toe or risk losing the foot*, was the essence of his deadly serious words. My spirits sank and my mind turned blue. *Why me?* I selfishly thought.

But then with a firm hand, Cambodia stood up. She reached back, and she slapped me appropriately hard.

To travel is to learn, not just that which we see in the sights around us, but also that we can on close examination, see in ourselves. Cambodia moved me in a way that made me not only examine the lives and the legacies I saw, but to look newly at my own as well. What arrogance, I realized it was, to feel self-pity and loss over a one-centimeter bone at the end of a truly expendable toe; so many people I had met in the months and years before in Cambodia, and Lebanon too, had lost one leg or both to landmines or unexploded ordnance, *UXOs*. I straightened my back, pushed my chin up, signed the medical authorization, and got on with the task at hand. *Cambodia with its sadness and its hope had taught me well.*

I am lucky to have worked and traveled in Cambodia many times. To have met its people, heard its troubles, felt its aspirations. I thank this country for the lessons I have learned at its hands. Having seen its best and heard its worst, I left *Phnom Penh* and Cambodia with sorrow. To paraphrase the sage and poetic Kahlil Gibran, I did *leave this city with a wound in my spirit*. But I also left with hope and joy. I feel fortunate to have seen the hard work and strong will of people reclaiming their dignity and their lives. I feel blessed to have found not just the horrors of its history, but to have also met Cambodians who embody the best of what their country can be. Though I left *with sorrow, with a wound in my spirit*, I left with happiness and hope as well. *Thank you, Cambodia, for the lessons you taught me. I wish you well.*

Big Brother and the Desert Mirage

Egypt (1996)

Beware the smoke and mirrors.

Tourist account of Las Vegas

I had just unlocked the door of my hotel room when the telephone rang. *Mohammed's* voice echoed at the other end of the line. He was five floors down.

"You didn't eat your dinner."

A shadow of my late mother looked down at me with a stern expression on her face. *Margaret, clean your plate.* Her face faded into *Mohammed's*; his dark eyes, tanned face, and his shadow of a beard watched me closely through the questions at the other end of the phone.

Excuse me?

"You didn't finish your rice. *Why not?* And you left your soup."

His words flew at me through the receiver in a surprisingly sharp and judgmental tone.

"I'm tired and I thought I was hungry but I'm not. Thank you for your concern. Good night."

Click. I hung up the phone.

Perhaps he was worried about my comfort in his country or in his hotel, but his call transported me decades into the past, making me feel like a newly-scolded six-year old. *Why didn't you eat your dinner?* His voice smacked of intrusion and reprimands and childhood places my psyche did not want to go. The room was still; the air was growing dim. A strange and heavy question mark hung annoyingly in the space around me. I crawled into bed and cracked open a book, escaping from and into the words of others until I fell asleep.

Two days before, I had arrived in Egypt in the very early hours of the day. I had come from Dubai on an Emirates Airlines flight. It was an up-to-date plane with comfortable seats, good food, and an attentive crew. A big change from my usual Third World haunts. By the time I arrived in Cairo, the airport was empty. The sky was dark save a few stars that flickered in the indigo void resting above my head. There was a chill in the mid-February air. A forty-five minute ride in the shadows of a well-worn cab took me out to the hotel, where metal detectors and an x-ray machine greeted me at the door. I walked into the lobby at ten past two a.m.

This was Egypt, a mythical and mystical place of pyramids and *pharaohs*, of deserts and camels, King *Tutankhamen*, dusty palms, and sweet-smelling, water-filled *hubba-bubba* pipes. A place of storybooks and history books and Hollywood. A place that was larger than life. Where young boys with firm voices far older than their years, a bluster of confidence, and a glint in their eyes command camels several times their size. Where the hustle and bustle of crowded markets takes on an exotic cast. Where tales of *Cleopatra's* beauty inspire historians, craftsmen, tourists, filmmakers, novelists, romantics, and peasants alike. And where wind-fed *feluccas* carry travelers, traders, and farmers back and forth over the muddy waters of the mighty Nile.

As I entered the lobby I somehow expected the butterflies in my stomach to instead flutter through the air, to see hotel staff with a spring in their step and a smile in their eyes. But at two in the morning, the few men on duty moved in slow motion like electric toys whose batteries were running low. I walked up to the reception desk and gave my name.

The world, already slow, came abruptly to a stop.

How did I get there? The night manager wanted to know, a look of shock on his face.

"I took a taxi. My plane was a few hours late."

In the flash of an instant, newly anxious staff in hotel uniforms started to scurry about, their batteries suddenly recharged.

"We're very sorry."

"Our driver thought your flight was cancelled."

Two members of the staff collided mid-air in their rush to come and apologize.

"Please, just give us a minute to double-check your room."

I, a foreign woman, had come alone to Egypt, to North Africa, to the Arab World, *to this Giza hotel.* Unaccompanied. *Alone.* In the middle of the night. Me. A woman. A foreign woman *by myself.*

When I exited the airport Immigrations desk and the hotel shuttle I had requested was not there, I simply found a public taxi and came to the hotel on my own. I had done the same many times before in many other countries in the middle of many other nights. I did not think it was a big deal. For the hotel staff though, it seemed to be a very upsetting thing.

They took my bag, poured me a refreshing glass of *Karkade*, a cold, sweet, red hibiscus drink, and they bumped into each other in their efforts to show me the way to my room. Within minutes I followed French vanilla pants, a burgundy tunic, black shoes, and very short, curly, black hair down the soft carpet and quiet hall. A hand in front of me turned the knob and gently pushed open the door. I stepped inside and stopped, speechless, my mouth open wide. My brain began dancing in excitement as my eyes adjusted to the marvels before me. It was not the breathtaking three-room suite they had upgraded me to, when I was booked at their cheapest rate. It was not the bowl of luscious tropical fruit. It was not the luxurious marble bath, or the rich Oriental rugs. There in front of me, pointing up in resplendent glory to the farthest reaches of the night sky, were the ancient pyramids of *Giza*, shimmering silvery-beige in the soft light of the February moon.

When I awoke six hours later the sky was hazy under the mid-morning sun. A translucent dust-colored blanket wrapped the late winter day. When I had cleared the shadows from my eyes, I looked out the wall-sized window of my elegantly appointed suite. The horizon was empty. The canvas before me was blank. In the silence of that February day, there was a gaping void where I was sure the pyramids once stood. They were gone. The grand pyramids I swore I had seen just a few short hours earlier had disappeared. Wiped mysteriously from the scene. There was neither a thin shadow nor a dark silhouette. Daylight had surreptitiously stolen the beautiful gilded image of my first Egyptian night.

Mirages in the desert are legendary. Illusions. Glistening images that summon us forth. Smoke and mirrors that tease us for a fleeting moment with what we want to see. Like a seductive mistress, they disappear as quickly and easily as they come, pulling back from outstretched arms, leaving nagging disappointment and hunger in their wake. Had I only been imagining the pyramids when I first arrived, over-anxious to see these well-documented wonders of the ancient world? Over the course of the day we would play an ongoing game of architectural *Hide and Seek* as they faded repeatedly in and out of the mid-February Egyptian haze.

There was a knock at my room. A splash of vibrant color greeted me as I opened the door. It was a man with a grand bouquet of fragrant fresh flowers and a request to meet with the General Manager of the hotel.

"Please accept our apologies," the G.M. said.

He offered me dinner at the *Giza* restaurant of my choice, and more and more flowers arrived in my room. It was fast becoming a deliriously colorful dream. Sure, they had failed to greet me at the airport and to drive me to the hotel in the luxury of a private van. But they had already apologized. They had upgraded me to this beautiful suite. They had sent me flowers, fresh fruit, Egyptian sweets. Now dinner, and flowers again, and again. They were trying in earnest to overcome their error, but this was getting to be *over the top*, as my friends from the United Kingdom would say. Much more than a simple mistake would usually warrant. *What was really going on?* I had to ask myself.

The notion of a woman traveling alone, as I most often do, is foreign in many parts of the world. An abstract concept that few can conceive and fewer can understand. *Had my husband given his permission for me to travel?* I am often asked, whether the one enquiring knows if I am married or not. *Am I not afraid to travel alone? Does it not make me lonely and sad? What if I get sick?* My solitary travels regularly meet with confusion, sadness, or concern. In socially conservative countries a woman traveling solo, by public buses and cabs, is a practice that just does not culturally exist. It is an idea whose time has not yet come. My arrival alone at the hotel late at night had clearly stirred the pot. But this was *Giza*, after all, a Westerners' tourist destination for easily more than a hundred years. Their concern was nice but it seemed all out of proportion to the minor inconvenience of taking a taxi by myself. I was surely not the first foreign woman to travel to this hotel alone, nor would I likely be the last. Perhaps I had misjudged the strength of societal norms and cultural dictates. I was perplexed. But I was learning, too, that nothing in this country was quite what I expected, nor was it ever quite what it seemed.

If it were not my culturally aberrant action of traveling by myself without the company or permission of a man that flustered the hotel staff, perhaps it was my physical safety that sat at the root of their concern. Even in early 1996, there were metal detectors at the hotel doors and an x-ray machine for everyone's bags. There had been bombs on the road to *Giza*. There had been tourist massacres down south. But would two foreigners rather than one attract less attention or more, even if one were male? In most places I go, I honestly believe I am safer alone than in a group and even safer than half of a pair; I believe that I am often safer abroad than on the college campuses of America, on many streets of my birthplace, the United States, or in the nooks and crannies of San Francisco, where I have lived, unafraid, for many years.

Maybe it was a simple but gracious belief in the importance of hospitality for a guest who has traveled great distances, who has come to visit from afar. Some could construe the hotel's failure to meet me with the scheduled greeting at the airport as an embarrassingly glaring lack of the warm and welcoming hospitality for which the Arab world is renowned.

Perhaps, it was merely economics at work, manifesting itself as a genuine concern about the experiences I would later recount to friends and family as I returned home. In a country heavily dependent on the six or more billion U.S. dollars a year that foreign tourists bring, the hotels had already seen revenues shrink severely with each new bomb, tourist massacre, and terrorist attack. Maybe my hotel was just doing its part to ensure that I, as one traveler going home to a rich country and relatively wealthy friends, would have a memorably good time, encouraging, it would be hoped, other tourists to come visit Egypt, too.

In fact, it was probably a delicate dance of all the above, the result of world politics, economics, culture, reputation, and humanity melded in a stew pot of concern. I really wanted to understand just what was going on. On the surface, it might not seem so important to know, but identifying what makes an impression on those around me helps, in many places I travel, to keep me safe. Figuring out the culture, the politics, the economics, the hot buttons, the *Achilles'* heel wherever I am may one day make the difference between getting a bullet in the bull's eye so often painted on my back, or not, between losing my life or staying safe.

The pyramids of *Giza* were beautiful, and the desert was calm, but after two days I wanted to move downtown. Closer to the museums, the markets, the coffee houses, the people, and the ordinary buzz of Egypt's everyday life. On a friend's father's recommendation, I moved to a suggested local hotel in the center of town to experience Egypt more as the locals do. *But be careful what you wish for; you might just get it*, it has been said.

On arrival, a blank face and bored eyes met me from behind a Formica counter of discolored cinnamon brown. Up on the first floor, the reception desk was a small room with shadowy walls, and a fixture of dark, numbered cubby holes filled with unused, antiquated skeleton keys. The man at the counter was a stocky Egyptian with short black hair that clung to his head in miniature *bouclé* waves. He wore a long, beige cotton *djellaba* tunic over an ordinary white shirt and dark brown pants. A circular crocheted prayer cap hugged the top of his head. I registered, and *Mohammed* gave me a key to a room up on the sixth floor. Little did I know that registering in this heretofore nameless, faceless, nondescript hotel was the start of an experience I would remember vividly for years to come.

The restaurant, *Mohammed* told me, was on the fourth floor and opened in the evening at seven. There were no stairs, he added. An arthritic elevator cage many times my age creaked and groaned as it labored to move me up and down. The second and third floors were locked; they did not belong to the hotel.

Like so many things in the developing world, this hotel was cobbled together from miscellaneous bits and pieces that do not quite match. Odds and ends force-fitted into one awkward unit where the whole is not greater than the sum of the parts, but rather it is less. Where one plus one does not add up to two, but rather to some inefficient, mismatched machine that leaves synergy a phantom dream, a make-believe concept that exists only in the wishful thinking of an educated few. This edifice exemplified the inefficiency that robs a population of the full potential of what its country could be. That leaves tourists frustrated. That leaves businesses falling ever farther behind in the global competitiveness of the world today.

I entered my room and locked the door. It was a small and simple space with rose-colored walls. A tired blue and brown flowered spread draped the sagging, double bed. Far above the dust and the din of the street, the room was clean and quiet and sported a peep hole in the door, a decent lock, and a good view from the window of the surrounding buildings and the streets below. As I looked out, a neighbor washed her laundry by hand in a yellow plastic tub on the roof-top across the way. Two children were playing tag one building over. Some men were playing cards. On the sidewalks below men with their briefcases and a few women in somber scarves walked briskly through their daily routines.

When the restaurant opened I rode the elevator down. At a square table with a grease-stained, white cotton cloth, I ordered the two meatless dishes the menu offered. A bowl of tomato soup and a plate of vegetable fried rice. After a long wait to the sound of tedious music that whined and groaned in a slow, sad stream, my food finally arrived. The rice was not fried. It had no bits of vegetable. No garlic or onion. No seasonings. Not even any *MSG*. It was a big plate of flavorless, plain, soft, boiled white stuff that demanded an acquired taste I have not yet found. It was not even close to the vegetable fried rice I had had envisioned in my mind. The soup was a smooth, translucent red liquid infused with a full shaker of salt.

Explain my disappointment or ask the waiter for a change? Our communication at the moment was challenged, at best. The waiter spoke almost no English, no *Bambara*, no Tajik, *Farsi*, and even less French. At that moment, that was pretty well the extent of my linguistic repertoire. My Arabic consisted *of hello, good-bye, my name is Margaret, thank you, Praise be to Allah, yes,* and *no*. I resigned myself to a hungry night, thanked the waiter, paid my bill, and left, going directly to my sixth floor room. It was then that *Mohammed's* telephone call came. *Big Brother* was watching, or rather *Mohammed* and the other hotel staff. *Madame you didn't eat your dinner* invaded my privacy, my quiet, my highly cherished sense of personal space.

I awoke early the following morning to the warm sun of an ordinary Cairo day, having forgotten the phone conversation of the evening before. I dressed and descended for breakfast. A friend was taking me sightseeing. Though I had not alerted *Mohammed* that I was going to dine downstairs, he told *Akram* I was in the restaurant for breakfast and he could meet me there, on the somber and lifeless fourth floor. After strong coffee and a few bites to eat we rode the lift to the sixth floor so I could grab some things from my room before we went down and out to go sightseeing for the rest of the day. *Akram* stood in the hall, moving one foot to hold open the door. No sooner had his shoe touched the floor, but my telephone rang.

"Hello?"

"*Madame. He cannot be in your room.* Your guest. He must come downstairs *immediately*." *Mohammed's* voice was cold and hard as steel.

"Good morning *Mohammed*. We were just picking up a few things. The door has stayed open, he is not in my room; he's just at the door, and we are leaving now."

The exchange had an uncomfortable, intrusive feel. It resurrected the call from the night before as it ripped holes in the shroud of privacy I wanted to believe cloaked me in my daily life.

We went out for much of the day. The museum filled my mind with the golden treasures of the *pharaohs'* time. The crowded markets satisfied my appetite for mingling with the locals and hunting for an exotic souvenir. A colorful horse-drawn carriage transported me down long, confusing Cairo streets where market stalls competed for a few square feet and pedestrians crowded the path. Two angry sixty-something-year old men heaving bright yellow bananas at each other after a loud exchange of words capped my entertainment for the day. I returned to my room. Quietly eating a late afternoon snack as I sat alone on my bed, I chose to skip dinner in the restaurant that night.

At about nine in the evening my telephone rang.

"*Madame*."

"Yes, *Mohammed?*"

By now I knew *Big Brother's* voice.

"You have not gone down to dinner. *Why not?*"

Does this man ever go off duty? Does he ever read a book, a newspaper, listen to the radio, or think about his family or friends instead of watching and worrying about me? Does he ever simply fall asleep and ignore the guests like so many developing world hotel receptionists, telephone operators, and security guards do? I was learning how violated I feel when that invisible sense of privacy and space is unilaterally torn away. I was also learning the hotel I thought would be a quiet, interesting little local place to stay felt instead like a den of spies.

I was beginning to question *Mohammed's* concern. How and why was he watching me on the fourth and sixth floors from his reception desk downstairs? Why did he care? How extensive was his surveillance? What else did he see? Who else was in on his game? I have been under a decidedly watchful eye in several countries. My phone was tapped in Tajikistan; my letters were often opened and read in Mali. In my early years in Viet Nam, the police regularly queried my neighbors and my office and field staff about my activities, my acquaintances, and my whereabouts. But it had never been thrown back in my face in quite such a constant and intrusive way. I had been cautioned in furtive whispers in Egypt about alleged secret police. I had initially given it little mind. But I was beginning to wonder if those warnings were true.

That evening *Akram*, his sister, and I went out into the Cairo night. I wanted to experience the night life and the evening celebrations of *Ramadan*. I also wanted a break from *Mohammed* and his overbearing, over-attentive, over-interested hotel and staff. People crowded the streets. The coffee houses were noisy and packed. The restaurants overflowed. It was the Muslim holy month of fasting, when the devout do not eat or drink from sunrise to sunset. It is a serious time of devotion and prayer, of inner reflection, a time for *Allah*. It is also a time for celebration at the end of each day. Once the sun sets, festive lanterns are lit in the streets of Cairo, signaling that people can break the religious fast with the *Iftar* meal. The crowds swelled. It was a joyous time for family and neighbors and friends. People dined, they visited, they socialized, they relaxed. We found a small food stall that still had a bit of room, and we enjoyed *falafel, foul*, rice, *hummus*, fresh sugarcane juice, and tea. Filling, flavorful staples of the Middle Eastern cuisine. I returned to my hotel room very late that night. For once *Mohammed* left me alone.

First thing the following morning though, I awoke with *Mohammed* weighing heavily on my mind.

"Do you still have a room available for the next nine days?" I asked.

I called my original *Giza* hotel and booked a room again, returning to my valued privacy and my quiet three-room suite. Maybe they, too, were watching my every move but at least if they were, they hid it well and in the process left me in ignorance and peace.

On the edges of town the color drained from view as a heavy layer of khaki covered the roads, the donkeys, the mud brick houses, the papyrus, the palm trees, and the sky. The world around me resembled a hand-painted, antique photo, the images a little fuzzy and dressed with just the thinnest wash of color, just the slightest hint of blue, ivory, ochre, and sage. Clear bright colors had long since faded, covered by the dust and washed out by the sun. It was an ordinary morning. Small shaggy pack mules plodded their daily route, carrying overflowing baskets and heavy sacks. Day laborers sat clustered in hopeful groups by the side of the road, tools in hand, waiting and wishing for a few hours of meagerly-paid work. Camels watched the world pass through half-closed eyes over pouting lips as they rested on accordion-folded legs. Occasionally one issued a loud sputtering snort. I checked back into my *Giza* hotel and dropped my bags, leaving again to search for the elusive pyramids. It was still early, about nine a.m.

There in front of me they stood in bold splendor. Three enormous sand-colored triangles against a sky of light, translucent blue. Two smaller ones quietly flanked one side. They had disappeared on me several times already in the recent past. Was I sure the pyramids were really there? *Now you see them. Now you don't.* It was a daily game of mystery, suspense, and surprise.

As the ancient pyramids stood before me tall and proud, I felt something that transcends my words. What is it about these simple structures that is so complex? What is it about these storied pyramids that lures people from around the globe? That speaks across vastly different cultures and across eons of time? That has withstood the cutting wind and the burning sun? That defies today's engineers with their degrees and their computers and their books? That is so mystical? So magical? So grand? These structures, with their magnificently simple faces stand their own against any other in the world. Against the carefully carved temples of India, or Cambodia's *Angkor Wat*. Against the shining gold domes of the pagodas in Myanmar. Against the Mayan ruins, I. M. Pei's extraordinary contemporary designs, the skyline of modern Shanghai, the *Tour Eiffel*. I toured the area and returned to my hotel to let the enormity of it all soak in.

Walking down the street the following afternoon another image caught my eye. The mahogany designs were striking. Delicate patterns on her palms, the back of her hands, running elegantly up her arms, well beyond her wrists. A sepia image, a dark nutmeg color on her light brown skin. In downtown Cairo I had silently admired this woman's beautifully hennaed hands. I, too, wanted to henna my palms. I asked the hotel staff in *Giza* for addresses and names of places where I could get it done. *Talk to the bellman this afternoon*, I had been advised. And so I did.

"Let me talk to my mother. She might do it for you."

The next afternoon I accompanied him home.

It was a quiet working-class neighborhood about a mile from the hotel. Drab-colored khaki-gray, one- and two-story, flat-topped houses and plain cement block walls lined unpaved, sand-colored streets. Young boys played soccer ambitiously in rising clouds of powdery dust. There was a beige-colored palm tree here and another tan-covered one there. And a lonely, dry scrub bush or two. A donkey ambled down the street. Another rested lazily by the side of the road, its matted coat caked with dried mud. *Abdul* opened the door and we stepped into the world inside.

"I'm going to show you my beauty first, my true love," he said.

Abdul's eyes grew soft and a warm, wistful smile slipped over his face. He opened another door and again led me inside to the musty smell of coffee-colored air and manure. He opened a window to give me more light.

Before me, chewing a mouthful of hay, stood *Abdul's* pride and joy. Magnificent mink-colored eyes fringed by long curling lashes looked me lazily up and down. A white dromedary the shade of fine raw silk, the softened white of antique ivory, she was relatively rare and highly-prized, a sizable investment for a hotel employee like *Abdul*. After kind words and loving pats on the head, we turned and climbed downstairs. *Abdul's* father had not yet brought his other camel home.

Upstairs I was introduced to *Abdul's* mother, his brothers, a cousin, a niece. This family lives on tourism. Like so many others in Egypt and elsewhere, they thrive on tourism, or they barely survive, depending on a cruel mix of exchange rates, airfares, politics, glossy magazine spreads, news reports, weather, the whims of the gods, and the anger and actions of the terrorists. *Abdul* and his brothers work in the hotels, completing miniscule salaries with precious tourist tips. Dad takes the visitors at the pyramids for a camel ride. Cousins sell souvenirs. When tourism is strong, *Abdul* and his relatives do well. When it plummets with each new terrorist event, this family and others suffer a heavy price.

I was installed in a lounging chair in a quiet room off to the side while the men performed their evening prayers. *Abdul's* mother joined me; quickly she went to work. As she chattered away in lively Arabic, I could only imagine what she said. She took hold of my hands and turned up my pale rose-colored palms. She pressed my fingers flat in the cradle of her own strong, thick hands. She rolled up my sleeves. And she brought out the pungent, pistachio-colored henna paste. I waited in anticipation as visions of sugarplums and graceful artwork danced in my head. I remembered the delicate copper patterns on the hands of the woman I had seen downtown, the fine lines and intricate paisleys and beautifully detailed leaves. I looked forward to watching how *Abdul's* mother would make the sophisticated designs. Would she use a fine pen-like style, a needle-less syringe, or a cook's pastry bag with a very fine tip?

She took my right hand in one of hers, and again she pressed my fingers flat. She reached for a slab of paste. Like a hungry diner with a thick slice of bread, soft butter, and a knife, she spread the henna on my opened palm. *Slap. Slap. Slap. Slap. Slap.* A thick green paste covered every centimeter of the flattened palm of my hand.

She took my left hand and swiftly did the same. She motioned for me to keep both hands outstretched, and then she left the room. Quickly she returned, brandishing two mint-colored plastic bags. She covered each hand and its henna in plastic and tied each bag with a knot at my wrist. She motioned for me to keep both hands stretched out straight in their makeshift mittens of plastic and paste. Then she departed again into the mystery of the other end of the house. There, alone with my thoughts, I sat.

Henna stains your skin everywhere it sits. My palms were covered solid, the henna pressed flat in a thick swath of grainy paste the texture of damp, sandy earth. *Beautiful, delicate, intricate designs as I had seen on the hands of the woman downtown?* Those visions faded like the lingering notes of a sad, sweet song. I waited in silent despair for thirty minutes or so, while the henna tarnished my skin, darkening my light palms to a solid, reddish-brown-black, as if I had carelessly polished my hands with dark *Kiwi* wax, instead of polishing my shoes. What I thought would be a work of art melted before my eyes into a cultural experience at which I could only shake my head and laugh. Like so much in this country, my henna turned out very differently than I had expected or I had planned. It seems the country folk of Egypt find the plain beauty of a solid color more appealing than fancy squiggles and flowers and paisleys and leaves. My stained hands were more *Daisy Mae* than *Harper's Bazaar*. Though it bore no resemblance to my ignorant expectations and hopes, I was getting a beauty treatment of unparalleled results that would take several very long weeks to fade.

"How is your henna?" *Akram* asked that night by phone, knowing what I had had in mind.

I could only respond with a laugh.

In fact, *Abdul's* generous invitation home was more than a trip to an impromptu and privileged private beauty salon. He had also invited me to join his family in breaking the *Ramadan* fast at the end of the day. In *Abdul's* home I shared the *Iftar* meal with his parents, his siblings, his cousin, and his niece. After the sun went down, the family had said their prayers, and my henna was set, we feasted on chicken, vegetable stews, *hummus*, rice, red hibiscus drinks, sweets, and fruit. They could not have shown me kinder hospitality and they asked nothing in return. Me, a stranger from far away. They asked if I had visited the pyramids. When I responded *yes*, *Abdul's* father told me that according to Egyptian legend, I must return to see the great Pyramids of *Giza* many times. Years later, I did just that.

At the end of a gracious evening, *Abdul's* father asked to take me the following morning to the pyramids on his son's white beauty, *Abdul's* great love and pride. It was his father's gift to me from Egypt, *Abdul* said, so I would not forget his family, his heritage, the beauty of his land. It was a lovely ride atop a striking and lovingly adorned beast. Colorful, hand-woven wool blankets and a carefully crafted leather saddle graced her white back. Yarn pompoms in navy, copper, hunter green, and rust hung from long woolen braids on her head. Across the sand and gravel we strode on long legs, heads held high. This was the Egypt of coffee table books, bright postcards, and colorful tourist brochures. Of movies and romantic dreams and childhood imagination. Yes, I should return to the pyramids many times.

Abdul intrigued me with the love he showed for his stately white beast. Never before had I seen such devotion for a seemingly common work animal, a beast of burden. Camels are notorious for their nasty tempers. They are the *Bad Boys* of the animal world. Handsome, romantic, endearing, but harboring a wild, unpredictable, irreverent, and tempestuous streak. Stories abound of these animals biting their riders or turning to jettison some maliciously targeted spit right onto whoever sits on their back. But this camel was the object of a genuine love affair.

131

Abdul's affection seemed unwavering, his reverence and devotion supreme.

Whether it is their drooping lids and big, gentle eyes, their slow, lumbering gait, or childhood tales asking *How the Camel Got his Hump*, something intrigues, puzzles, captivates me about these animals. I hired a car and driver and left for the camel market, ninety minutes outside of town. Past dusty villages, barren earth, and blowing sand. Past flat horizons, gripping poverty, and cruelly arid land. Awaiting me, at the end of the road, was one big patch of scorched, dry dirt, a parking lot with dromedaries as far and wide as the eye could see.

There were dark animals the color of Turkish coffee. There were camels the color of golden caramel, with patchy, moth-eaten coats. There was the occasional white beauty that was handled tenderly, with great respect and care. One old grandfather labored to take each painful step, white foam bubbling forth from his tired and sagging mouth. A baby stood by its mother's side, wobbling on very unsteady legs. Most of the animals were hobbled, one leg bent at the knee and tied at the ankle so they could walk slowly and unevenly on three legs but could not run. Small clusters of men sat in the shade and a few stood about under the morning sun; I watched as they haggled over prices, showed their stock, smoked hand-rolled cigarettes, and just patiently passed the time of day. Buyers checked ivory teeth, strong bites, and scuffed hooves. Occasionally someone sent a camel unhobbled for a run through the lot to check his gait and his speed. Men from Egypt, Chad, Kenya, Libya, Algeria, and The Sudan milled about. Men who had traveled for days to buy and sell. *Tuaregs* stood wrapped in blue, with gauze turbans twisted systematically about their heads. Egyptians in long *djellabas* and crocheted prayer caps. Young peasant boys with bare feet and unkempt, dust-covered hair. There was not another woman within miles, but I was in my element, at peace in the desert sand.

After a full morning of watching the camels and the traders and meandering through the market, my driver and I departed. *Foreigners are crazy*, he must have thought, as I took incomprehensible delight that morning in the camels and the merchants and the dust.

It had been a series of lessons in the unexpected, my vacation in this dusty, hazy, exotic corner of the ancient world. But before I left, Egypt held out for me one final surprise. One more shimmering, captivating, seductive, and romantic gift. One more desert mirage. Awaiting me back at the hotel when I returned was one more very extraordinary bouquet of flowers. Eighteen beautiful red roses from *Akram*. He phoned and invited me to the Nile for a sunset *felucca* ride. There, with great ceremony and romance, *Akram* asked me for my hand. Promising me a lifetime commitment and undying love, he asked me to marry him. There, in a small boat on the great Nile, as the sun was going down. We had met earlier in another country, on a different continent, in a very distant place. And now in Egypt, an ancient place that had stood the test of adversity and time, he promised me enduring love and timeless devotion.

My time in Egypt was drawing to an end; I am not sure what I was looking for, but over and over again what I found was different than it first appeared; it was different than I initially thought. In the end, Egypt was for me a land of illusions, of the unexpected, of things that seductively offer tantalizing promises, of images and dreams that do not last. It is the birthplace of the desert mirage. So many things I found in Egypt were not what I first thought they would be. While they were interesting, memorable, endearing, confusing, humorous, romantic, they parted more easily than they came. Only the memories, the stories, and one photograph from Egypt have stood the test of time. A remembrance of faces and actions and experiences and words, of promises, of scenes, and sounds, and flavors, and smells. Of Egypt, just the memories remain.

And so, I was reminded that in life, promises may fade, people and circumstances may disappoint, but I have learned that I will always have my stories, my mental images, my memories. Those will always be mine.

Beware the land of illusions. *Beware the smoke and mirrors.* Beware the desert mirage.

Lost and Found at 10,000 Feet

Costa Rica (2000)

We don't receive wisdom.
We must discover it ourselves after a journey
that no one can take for us or spare us.

Marcel Proust

Strength. Courage. Wisdom. Safety. I wanted badly to quit. My lungs burned, my thighs screamed, my calves cramped and my feet ached. I fought with myself about whether to stop. I was cold and tired and dirty and wet. I wanted, more than anything, to give up. I was often thrown off-balance by the uneven earth, the grease-like mud, and the weight of the pack on my back. I slipped on wet leaves. I learned anatomy as I pulled muscles I did not know I had. I had known in advance that this trek would be hard. That is why, in fact, I had signed on. But it was *hard*. It was *brutally* hard. *Discouragingly* hard. Almost impossibly hard.

It was tempting to make a deal with the devil, but I could not, I would not, I did not let myself down. *Strength. Courage. Wisdom. Safety.* I made these words my mantra, my personal Buddhist chant. I repeated them over and over and over again, more than a thousand times a day. I repeated them silently to the exclusion of all else, making a commitment to myself to allow no other thoughts rented space in my brain. *Strength. Courage. Wisdom. Safety.* Take another step. *Strength. Courage. Wisdom.*

Safety. One more meter. *Strength. Courage. Wisdom. Safety.* Up the next hill. Again and again the voice in my head echoed my silent, very private, very personal *mantra.* My own very personal chorus. My own very private chant.

I had camped solo without a tent in the sub-zero February snow and solitude of northern Minnesota and I had survived. I had run a marathon in Bangkok's humidity and heat; I have the medal to show. I had served two years in Africa as a Peace Corps Volunteer. I had beaten malaria that haunted me in the darkness of the night. I had beaten dysentery in the desert. But nothing had adequately prepared me for imitating a pack mule in the mountainous cloud forest of Costa Rica, on a very long and torturously winding trail. When friends ask me, with excited anticipation in their voices, how I liked Costa Rica, they expect me to chatter enthusiastically about birds and beauty and the magnificence of the mountains and the plants and the trees. But my reaction is always the same. My mouth opens. I start to speak. But the words catch, unspoken, in my throat.

We assembled in a mid-city youth hostel the night before. Ten or twelve or fourteen of us. I have since lost count. Fifteen- and sixteen-year olds, two twenty-one year-olds, a twenty-two year-old, plus two very young guides. And me. I could have been everyone's mother. If I had started having children early, I could have been their grandmother. It was them, and me, and ten infinitely long days in the woods.

We got off to an early start, leaving the *San José* hostel for a crowded, noisy bus station at the crack of dawn. Backpacks, food, matches, pots, pans, sleeping bags, maps, flashlights, a machete, and a tarp. I should have taken heed and turned back when, as we walked down the sidewalk, someone two floors above opened the window and heaved the dirty dishwater. It landed squarely on my head. I should have recognized that omen for what it was. We were just getting started, but it only went downhill, or rather uphill, from there.

We climbed by public bus through the early morning mist. It was a hazy, dreamlike sort of ride. Everyone was quiet. Most were asleep. I was alone with my thoughts. *What lay ahead?* I wondered as I watched the fog-shrouded scenery roll by. It had been a trying several months of going through a painful divorce that led me to my decision to take this challenge on. Now I was about to be put to the test.

Just after ten in the morning and ten thousand feet up, the scratched and dented bus ground to a cranky halt at the muddy edge of the road, sputtering a tubercular cough into the thin mountain air. Some people stretched. Others muttered incoherently. Everyone groaned. We disembarked in slow motion, none of us eager to alight. The sky was dull; the air was cold. The weather was damp and gray. A drizzle started, light at first then growing to a short but steady rain. It was the beginning of a bad dream; this trek was just commencing, but it was not looking good.

After a light snack of raisins and bright-colored *M&Ms* we threw our packs on our backs and headed up a ragged, narrow, rock-studded trail. Not only had I been living at sea level in the tropics for the previous twelve months, but at my lowest adult weight, I shouldered a pack that easily figured more than sixty percent of my own body weight. Meanwhile, my companions were bright-eyed, athletic, young things, full of energy, high on life, hormones, and youth. We were not well matched. To say it was challenging for me would be an understatement of enormous magnitude. I was determined, though, to do my share and to pull my weight, as farther and farther up the mountain we climbed.

The sky was dark and the trees were still when we started out each day. Even the ants and the spiders continued to sleep. We crawled only under agonizing duress from the warmth and relative comfort of the sleeping bags that were our nylon and polyester cocoons. Murder would have been kind if it had saved me from putting on my cold, wet clothes in the frigid mountain air. On those mornings, *Ben Gay* became my masseuse, my savior, my lover, my closest friend. When my muscles were tight, my legs ached, and my shoulders and back complained, the penetrating heat of that mentholated cream was worth more to me than money or gold.

When I think of Costa Rica in my mind today, I do not see the emerald leaves, or the vines that climb lightly with an acrobat's strength and agility and grace. I do not see the brilliant feathers of the *Toucan*, or the tropical iridescence of a butterfly's wings. I do not hear the light melody that floats through the air like a Venetian waltz or the clear call of a parrot. I don't see the monkeys play. I do not feel the softness of a thick, protective cloud, or the crystalline power of a thousand drops of rain. I see only a translucent blur of watery green and brown.

We hiked single file through the dense foliage, along a very narrow path that at most times we could barely see. Up and down, down and up. Six to nine hours a day. Like the strong *Leaf Cutter* ants we watched in great admiration and awe, we marched relentlessly forward carrying disproportionately large loads on our backs. One after the other, nose to tail, nose to tail. Through wet green leaves and slick brown mud and the smell of rich, wet earth. We climbed over slippery rocks and fallen trees. At a pace that made my lungs struggle and my head hurt. That made my knees quiver and my arms shake. The branches whipped our bodies and slapped our cheeks. Pain and fatigue pelted my brain. Like masochists in some off-color scene, we were willing partners in this dark game. *I paid well, and of my own volition, for this?* I must have been stark-raving mad, I thought on more than one occasion. *Strength. Courage. Wisdom. Safety.* Three more steps. As we hiked on and on, each eternal minute for me lasted an hour, each hour lasted a day.

"*You can't stop!*" Will turned around to me and said with glaring eyes and a cutting edge to his voice. There was fire in his tone.

"*You have to move faster. You're slowing us down,*" Will said, though I was not alone at the back.

My blood pressure climbed as my determination fought hard against my muscles' near-debilitating fatigue. At a very young sixteen years old, Will had no idea the discouraging force his sharp words hurled my way. We were still two miles higher than I had been for years and the low oxygen and heavy pack were taking an enormous toll. And in reality, this was to be a challenging exercise, not a forced march or a race through the woods under a veiled threat from someone not even half my age. Though I wanted badly to throttle this young man, I took a deep breath and quietly reminded him that this was to be a challenge for us all. For some, it was physically tough. Perhaps for those who moved with relative ease, the challenge was not physical, but one of patience and empathy. Will didn't speak to me again. *For the remaining eight or nine days.*

Making camp at night came to me as a surprisingly welcome chore despite the long and trying days. Once we set up our tarp and laid our sleeping bags out, the cutting, slicing, chopping, and stirring for our dinner was therapeutically meditative for me. While others tried to dodge their duty in the makeshift kitchen each night, I was happy to take my turn to cook and clean. There, if not on the trail, I could very easily hold my own.

Knowingly, we marched each day through the brush-covered territory of the venomous *Fer de Lance*, a notoriously deadly snake. We made our beds each night on the damp, leaf-covered, rock-strewn ground that was also home to poisonous frogs, spiders, and bugs. But I slept soundly at night in my sleeping bag on a plastic sheet on the cold, hard earth. I was simply too profoundly tired to care. Once horizontal, I dropped off so fast into a drug-like state, I risked missing the whispered good-nights of the rainforest, the joy of lying horizontal, the soothing darkness of the end of the day. Sleep came to me blessedly each night with lightening speed.

In fairness, it was not *all* torture and pain. There were occasional flickering moments of pleasure or silliness or fun, like when I slipped and fell, bouncing twenty feet down the muddy path on nothing more than the seat of my pants. Like when we passed a family of cinnamon-colored monkeys playing childlike overhead. When we found an unusually-colored flower, and a giant brownish-green frog. When we ate rice and black beans in a *shaman's* house, with an exceptional cilantro sauce. When we repelled down a thundering hundred-foot waterfall and we climbed an eighty-foot tree.

But for me, at least, there were also moments of sheer, almost paralyzing terror. When we reached a rockslide that had obliterated part of the already very narrow trail, on a particularly treacherous ring around the upper reaches of a bare mountain, my heart pounded, my legs stopped dead, and tears welled up in my eyes; a very deep-seated fear of falling reared its ugly head. I had no choice but to clench my jaw, move forward, and cross the unstable rocks, but I was overwhelmingly grateful for the sympathetic reach of an open hand. I may never fully get over the childhood afternoon I was pushed down a set of stairs, but at least now my fear of falling seems to kick in a little bit less.

Though we started at ten thousand feet and hiked up from there, we gradually came back down. All the way down to the sea. As the days wore on the hike grew less taxing. Ironically, as I acclimated to the altitude, we descended, climbing lower each day. As we ate our food, we lightened our packs. As we stressed our legs, my muscles grew strong. It all pulled together to form something of a hard-won victory and a very welcome reprieve.

Crocodile Mile, the rescue kayakers called it, having seen the quiet movement of the menacing jaws of the cold, calculating reptiles more than once. After ten days of hiking we reached a river. We threw off our packs, loaded the rafts, stripped down to swimsuits, donned life vests, and climbed aboard. Two and a half days of white-water rafting stood between us and the end of this trip. After the grueling rainforest hike, even the Class Four rapids in the bend in the river near where the crocodiles lived were like a delicious bit of rest.

Gliding in our rafts over gentle water that flowed like ribbons fluttering in a breeze gave us a respite from the labors of the previous ten, challenging days. I could feel both my body and my mind relax. During those moments, the water gods treated us well.

Flying through the boiling rapids where spirits danced and fought, foam washed our faces, and waves drenched our bodies, broke any monotony that threatened where the river was calm. The rapids sent our adrenalin racing; they made our hearts pound and our blood pressure soar. The *Urban Cowboy* and his mechanical bull had nothing on us as whirlpools and rocks sent us into watery spasms that jerked our heads in one direction and our legs in another, making us, at that moment, little more than a collection of flailing body parts and oars. I held on tightly to the thin safety cord as we traversed angry rapids that boiled and churned like the tortured dreams of a tormented mind, demonized by the boulders and empty pockets lying in the darkness below.

The alternating exhilaration and peace of the river shook loose any vestiges of frustration and fatigue, leaving me feeling energized, refreshed, renewed. Unlike the relief I felt at stepping out of the rainforest three days before and taking off my pack, I was sad to leave the river that had become my newest home away from home.

We were supposed to have a closing ceremony around a campfire our next to the last night. But the firewood was too wet and a light mist was falling, so our campfire became a pile of flashlights switched on and turned every which way. They sent their yellow-white beams of light in the different directions we would soon each go. It was supposed to be a time to share, a time to reflect. A time to think about what we had learned. We each received a malachite cloud forest frog with some Costa Rican significance, though I was so exhausted, I don't remember what. I had finally put my mantra to rest, but my brain was too tired to think.

"You earned this frog," one of the sixteen-year old boys said in a soft, measured voice. "Because you are the same age as my mother."

He looked into my tired eyes, and he paused.

"I cannot imagine her even *thinking* of doing something like this, much less finishing it with us. *But you did.*"

I could not find any words to express what I felt.

143

When we returned to *San José* after two weeks that felt like two years, we went back to the same downtown youth hostel where we had met that now distant first night. It was there, on wooden bunks in a cluttered room, that we were to spend our last Costa Rican night. After camping in the cloud forest without even the walls of a tent, and after enjoying the river's wide, free, open expanse, the hostel had a noisy, unsettling, and claustrophobic feel.

"How's the hot water?" someone called.

We had returned in dirty clothes, still covered with two weeks' sweat and mud. I waited quietly while others took their showers first. They were in a hurry to go out on the town. I was content to stay back and rest.

"It's cold," came the response.

In less than a minute I was on a pay phone talking to the five-star Intercontinental Hotel that I knew was just across town.

"Yes. We would be delighted to have you."

I said quick farewells and caught a cab. Looking like a rat the cat dragged in from the alley, I entered the elegant lobby still covered with mud. Heads turned. I looked more suited to a flop house or a detox clinic than the reception area of a beautiful luxury hotel. But I went to the desk and gave them my name.

"We've been expecting you. We have a very lovely room prepared."

Having climbed the ladder of their guest loyalty program really paid off that night. Within minutes of my arrival I had booked a massage, sent the entire contents of my backpack to the laundry, and given my boots to the bellman to clean. I had opened the bottle of wine they gave me, and ordered a room service meal I didn't have to cook. I slipped into the luxurious, bubbling water of a big, clean *Jacuzzi* in the privacy of my own bathroom, where a soft, clean, white robe and fluffy slippers lay in wait. My aches and pains melted away and the grime ran down the drain. A warm, down-filled bed called my name in the *Presidential Suite*. Sometimes there *is* justice in the world.

We do not receive wisdom. We must discover it ourselves after a journey no one can take for us or spare us, Proust said. This Costa Rican odyssey was a journey no one could have taken for me. In the wet and the mud and the leaves and the cold of the cloud forest I learned how far perseverance and determination can take me. No one could have taught me that. I learned that I am stronger than I sometimes think I am, and I rebuilt the confidence that in my divorce I had temporarily lost. No one else could have done that for me. I discovered that the one who sets boundaries for me is often myself. No one else could have convinced me of the same. I learned that fear can be overcome. I learned that great physical exertion during the day can make even the rocks under my body feel sweet at night. But I also learned that a warm bath and a soft bed at the end of a long day are still a very welcome treat.

Riches That Money Can't Buy

The Ivory Coast (1992)

Rich are they in wonders seen.
But poor in the goods of men.

Rudyard Kipling, *The Sea Wife*

Raffia spun around me in a whirling, dizzying blur, in a warm blend of rustling brown and gold. Under the heat of the mid-afternoon sun broad shoulders cloaked in simple tunics of bold prints dipped and turned in tall, one-legged pirouettes, defying the laws of physics, gravity, nature, and man. Dark, muscular shoulders glistened with sweat. Wooden faces painted white, with eyes black like coal, spoke of mystery and religion that hailed from several generations past, from the thick forests and secret societies of West African indigenous culture and lore.

The sound of strong, steady fingers and the firm beat of a well-placed palm arose from goatskins stretched tight over homemade, hand-carved drums. A rich echo marched through my head. Its rhythm called my name. With resounding force it reverberated in the hollows of my chest, in the blood flowing through my arms and my legs. It made my head bob in time; my foot tapped the dirt. The drum's timbre stirred the men and women around me. Each firm strike of a hand stoked a fire in their eyes and roused embers deep within; their collective pulse riveted the air. The sound of the drums animated the figures before me, marking time for the remarkable movement in front of my eyes. Dips and whirls, extraordinary leaps, deep sweeping bows. These masked dancers transformed the patch of hard-packed earth into a grand stage of world class. Towering ten feet above the ground, culture danced in the warm, humid air and open dust of this tiny village in western *Côte d'Ivoire*.

The transit station was not for the faint of heart. It was not for the timid or the shy. Even for an intrepid traveler it required a certain focus and resolve. As the scratched and dented bus ground to a halt on the loose gravel and dirt, the quiet passengers that had so patiently ridden several hours from the last big town transformed into a heaving mass with a life of its own, every man and woman and child pressing toward the door. Gone was the politeness, the *politesse*. Gone was the easy attitude, the warmth West Africans commonly show. In its place roared a primitive urge no less strong than that of a salmon driven to swim upstream in an ancient biological call. Crossing my arms over my chest, I double-checked the money pouch and passport I had already secured inside my shirt; I put my sunglasses away.

With a firm hold on the backpack that I had swung in front, I steeled my reserve and climbed down the steps of the bright blue breadbox on wheels. Into the throbbing crowd of hard-pressed bodies, of shouts and calls, into the swarm of bright cottons, dark faces, *espresso* eyes, mirrored sunglasses, of heat, humidity, blazing sunshine, and glistening sweat. I continued to hold my pack tight as firm bodies in colorful clothes pushed and shoved. Sharp voices shouted my way, above the chaos and noise.

"*La Française!*" *French woman.*

"*Madame! Ici! Venez avec moi.*" *Here! Come with me.*

"*White woman. Where do you want to go? I will take you there.*"

No time wasted even on the usual *I want to be your friend*, with its underlying hint of unfettered anonymous sex.

"Come with me," the voices called.

I was their would-be prize. Of a bus full of people, I was the one the taxi drivers wanted. I was the foreigner. The rich one. Like a movie star chased by the *paparazzi*, I was the object of their desire. They were not the object of mine.

Nothing stopped the hands from reaching for my pack in a belief that where it went I would follow, too. Strong fingers tried to grab my arm, my hand. But I, too, pressed firmly through the crowd, ignoring the calls, the shouts, the pulling, the pleas, my arms still tight around my navy-colored pack, my fingers laced in front. Experience had taught me in the months before that hesitation in bus and taxi stations was the invitation to a feeding frenzy by the taxi drivers, the peddlers, the touts. No less than hungry *piranhas* on an unfortunate, unwitting fish. Hesitation, even the slightest pause, would not get me where I needed and wanted to go and indeed might carry me along a path I did not want to follow, swept up by the strong currents of a driven crowd. Uncompromised focus and undeterred drive, instead, would serve me best.

I had just arrived in *Abidjan*, a heaving, teeming city fourteen million strong. Home to Alpha Blondy and his politicized reggae songs. *Wari Bana. The Money's All Gone.* The 1990s pop hit could be a national anthem for the continent as a whole. *Abidjan.* Once the pride of the French, with its successful businesses, modern buildings, relatively chic restaurants, and smart fashions. *Abidjan.* The commercial center of the Ivory Coast. A city which, after the villages of West Africa, looked like Los Angeles with its high-rises, new cars, and slick highway overpasses. But where a crazy man walking nude down the paved city street did not turn anyone's eye.

I made it to the shared-taxi stand where I secured a ride and headed west toward the Liberian border. Toward the sunset I rode over uneven pavement in a wreck on wheels with a driver in a race against time. He was an agitated man who had never taken a road test in his life, probably bought his driver's license on the street, and had no concept of risk or the value of life – either his, or mine. This was 1992 in *Côte*

151

d'Ivoire, once considered West Africa's jewel. This was before the civil war that started up north and rumbled south, steamrolling values and buildings and traditions and lives. The war that fueled hatred and fear. That raped and pillaged and murdered just to make a political point. That hurled bullets and knives and machetes through the air. That brought a country and an economy to its knees, though it was once one of Africa's bright stars. Like a meteor, this country shot across the sky in a brilliant flash before it crashed and burned on the ground.

Hours later and close to the rugged Liberian line, I found a small, twelve-dollar room for the night in a missionary lodge. It was a clean and modest place, safe and convenient, and the price was right at the time. There I slept in peace.

Hungering the next morning to leave the hard pavement and unremitting noise of the crowded cities and towns, I found a local boy for a guide. At ten years old, *Daouda* knew the mountain like the back of his hand. But of equal importance to me, he had not yet felt the testosterone surge that in my global observation haunts nearly every eleven-year old male. Hormones that fuel attitude with which I, at least, did not want to contend. Chemicals that drive a need to impress, an urge to show off. Traits I did not want leading me through the remote, unknown, snake-infested woods of a foreign land.

For the better part of the day, *Daouda* and I climbed the mountain, *Le Dent, The Tooth*. We hiked through thick, silent clusters of vine-covered trees, over fallen logs, through deep piles of damp leaves, up and down a twisted path. Under the watchful eye of mist-filled clouds and blue-white skies we trooped in the wet heat of a West African June. We passed the translucent gray fog of a thousand mosquitoes. We stepped over the hidden dens of venomous snakes. We trudged through humidity you could cut with a knife. Iridescent black beetles crossed our path. Spindly-legged, ash-colored spiders skittered over the earth before my feet. And *Army* ants formed a sharp black line in the dirt. We climbed until we reached the stunning views of the land down below, its green-leaved clusters the texture of giant *chenille*. After the crowded transport and *Abidjan's gare*, it was good to touch nature and leave man and his hardened, black asphalt far behind.

The mountain hike was superb. The air was quiet; the path was serene. The climbing exercised my legs; the stillness calmed my soul. But I had come to this region with another, loftier goal in mind. To find culture. To witness tradition. To visit *Zala*, a small rural village in the West. It was there, before me, that the masked dancers on six-foot stilts leapt and whirled and jumped to the rich sound of the deeply resonating drums.

I had found a ride to *Zala* with a missionary couple who generously shared space in their car. We had driven the main highway north to the turnoff point, and then headed fourteen kilometers east. Over an undulating path of gravel that traversed gently rolling hills and passed through quiet forested land. Though we felt quite smug in our venture into the unknown, we really were just three more in a long string of tourists who show up for a performance of the masked dancers. We were, though, the only ones that sunny June afternoon. Our enquiries met with a polite welcome and a positive response, followed by the missionaries' agreement on a small fee. In minutes we were seated in a clearing in the middle of a collection of huts. The drumming soon began.

For forty-five minutes masked figures danced in costume on six-foot stilts. The performance was riveting. Straight out of *The Discovery Channel*, it was an amazing exhibition of physical prowess, theatrics, and music. But despite our romantic notions, we were not the first to witness a little-known cultural event deep in the untouched bush. The rather arrogant myth of discovery we three foreigners wanted to believe dissolved in the reality of a commercial event when at the end someone passed a well-worn basket for tips.

Zala was an African picture from a coffee table book. A clean and quiet group of thatch-roofed, mud brick huts set in a small clearing among tall trees. The villagers were modest and polite. Their warm smiles and engaging eyes communicated friendliness beyond spoken words. The Chief spoke *Djoula*, a close cousin to the *Bambara* I knew, and he spoke a bit of French. As we prepared to leave this gentle village of mud and dust and straw in the middle of the forest in the mountain's shadow close to the Liberian border, *Zala* called my name.

N b'a fe ka sununke i ka dugula. Could I stay the night in his village? I asked the Chief.

They had had hundreds of foreign visitors over the years, he said.

Many people came to see the dancing, *Zala's* amazing acrobats on stilts. *Many foreigners come and they watch and they pay and they go.*

Only once before in his long years, recounted the Chief, *had anyone asked to stay. It was a white man a few years before.*

They would be honored by my visit, he said.

For all their talk of being one with the local people, of embracing local culture and folk, the missionaries looked quite disturbed by my news.

Was I really sure I wanted to stay? Would I be safe? Where would I sleep? How would I get back out the following day?

I insisted I would be fine and they left me there. No amount of money could buy what came next.

The village Chief showed me the way to a hut. His wife followed quickly with a clean sheet for the lumpy mattress on the institutional metal frame bed. They told me to leave my things and come with them. Obediently, I did as they said.

I followed the Chief back to the clearing where we had first been, and someone brought two discolored white plastic chairs. One for the Chief, and the other for me. The villagers wandered back in, slowly taking places behind me and to my side in the unhurried way of a people who have far more time than money, for whom minutes really just stand still.

Men returned with their musical instruments. Fingers began to pummel the skins tightened over the head of each hand-carved wooden drum. A low percussion started. Resembling the distant announcement of an approaching train, it grew gradually from a soft drone to a deafening roar. It grew from a light beat into a deep crescendo that filled the early evening air. Like that train rolling forward, rhythm traveled outward from the bellies of the leather-bound wood to fill the clearing around me with a thunderous call, punctuated artistically by space and time. Firm. Deep. Solid. And rich. The echo was loud and strong.

Then one figure burst forward in a cloud of dust, stopping abruptly within inches of my feet. In one swift, circular motion his carved, white face swooped down to within breathing distance of mine. He paused just an instant, looking deep into my eyes. Then just as quickly as he bowed low to the ground, he swiftly leapt backwards into the clearing to again stand straight and tall, a mysterious, muscular figure on six-foot legs.

Then out came another figure. And another. And another. And still one more. Soon a group whose skill and theatrics rivaled the best professional dancers I have ever seen was leaping and swirling in front of my eyes. Equal to any foreign dance troupe, any national ballet, any professional acrobats I have seen across the globe. I sat speechless as these artists, these athletes, these dancers flashed just heartbeats away from me, in a blur of color and balance and strength. Mystery and masks and motion blended in the cloud of dust that was once an empty space. Whirling around like spinning tops. Bending low then stepping high. On one leg, then on the other. All while balanced skillfully atop six-foot poles, with bodies cloaked in raffia skirts and cotton cloth, and faces masked in carved wood and rustling straw. Strong rhythm, steady balance, great agility, strength, and speed. A breathtaking performance, it was my own private, West African *Cirque de Soleil*. They danced for more than an hour. It was my own personal, incredible, unparalleled show. And no one passed a hat. No one passed a basket. No one asked for a tip.

That night the Chief's wife cooked dinner for me. Rice and a vegetable sauce. She heated a bucket of bath water on a wood fire and made sure I had a towel. Behind a woven thatch wall I washed, pouring dippers of warm water in satin ribbons over my back, under the cover of a star-lit sky. The Chief's son had given me his house for the night. It was a simple, one-room mud-brick building with a corrugated metal roof. The Chief made sure I knew how to fasten the latch on the silvery sheet metal door.

Kan kelen kelen wuli, people said. *May you awaken one by one.*

Villagers across Africa know that awakening suddenly and in unison is not a desirable thing. Rather it is the hallmark of a tragedy befallen their community, a catastrophe visited on them during the night. Much better to awaken individually, each in his own time.

Kan kelen kelen wuli, they say. *May you awaken one by one.*

Well-fed, happy, and clean, I slept deeply and awakened early, to the gentle light of a fresh new day. Just as she had prepared dinner for me the evening before, the Chief's wife had cooked a rice gruel when morning came. After the rice and a fresh banana from a village tree, it was time for me to go. A fourteen-kilometer hike over a lonely road stood between me and my next ride toward home. Fourteen kilometers on foot just to the pavement. Then several more miles stood before me and the nearest town that might have a shared taxi to carry me to the next bus station. The villagers bade me a warm farewell. It was time for me to leave.

In the gracious West African tradition, my host said farewell by *showing me*, his guest, *the road*. Walking to the edge of the village with me, the Chief thanked me for my visit and wished me safe travel. His son then joined me to accompany me further on my way. In all, the Chief's son walked six or seven kilometers with me before turning back, leaving me to continue only half the distance alone. What remained once he parted was a quiet, meditative walk, its solitude broken only by the sound of my feet on the gravel and a stop at a road-side pump to refill my water bottle. It was nice to be alone with my thoughts as I walked along the straight, gravel road. From the junction with the main highway, it was only minutes before the back of a bright red motorcycle carried me to the next taxi *gare*.

Across this part of Africa people will tell you it is forbidden to take photographs of masked dancers and that if you do so anyway, something bad will follow. Local people will tell you repeatedly that the dancers will not appear in the photos, but will be replaced on paper with a dark spot in the film. Or they will warn some other sort of unfortunate, unplanned occurrence will take place. I know many Westerners who have ignored the warnings, but with I do-not-know-what-results. I, however, always first asked permission to take photos of the dancers I saw, and it was never declined.

Three times in West Africa I witnessed the spectacle of an authentic, traditional masked dance. Three times I had permission from the village elders and the dancers themselves to take as many photos as I wished. And three times my photos failed. Those I took in *Zala* did not turn out. Months later, watching different masked dancers in *Bamako*, my camera jammed. The third time, when I went to pick up the developed pictures of extraordinarily close photos I had taken of the masked *Dogon* dancers further north, I was told by the San Francisco photo development lab that there had been no film in the canister I had left. Perhaps a stock shop now has my images for sale. *Or perhaps what the villagers say is true.*

If not in my photo album, those villagers found a special place in my memories and my heart. They became gracious, if accidental, hosts when I arrived unexpectedly from nowhere, at their door, and asked if I might stay. They took me in without hesitation but with unbounded generosity and warmth. They housed and fed me, entertained me, and gave me warm water to bathe, looking for nothing in return but the simple price of friendship, the pleasure of a few shared hours and a couple of shared meals. They entertained me in a priceless fashion, without asking me to pay. In our Western haste and hurry, I submit that we do not know what humanity and generosity we have lost.

I cannot imagine a stranger showing up in America at my door, having simply read about my neighborhood in a *Lonely Planet* travel guide. I cannot imagine him or her asking to stay for the night. But even harder is it for me to imagine opening my door without question, and kindly saying *yes*, to someone I do not know. I, who have the means to shelter and feed a stranger knocking at my door, would be the one to pause, not these impoverished villagers who have barely the equivalent of two nickels to their name.

The people of *Zala* wore simple clothes, their houses were small huts, their material possessions were modest and few. They had little of material wealth. They were, as Rudyard Kipling's words say, *poor in the goods of men*. But their culture, their tradition, their spirits, their hospitality, their humanity were rich, well beyond any cash in my pocket or any words I can write.

When I think today of the several times I traveled through The Ivory Coast, *la Côte d'Ivoire*, I remember the buses, the guest houses, the shared taxis, the rice and sauce. I remember the skinny little French priest who had just been mugged in *Abidjan* in the bright light of day. I can still see the extravagance of the Basilica in *Yamoussoukro* and hear its choir joyously filling the air. I recall the hand-weavers, the wood carvers, the metal workers, the hike in the mountains, and *Daouda* who at ten years of age served as my very able guide. I can still taste the fresh sweet juice from a coconut cracked open on the beach. But it is those dancers and those villagers, the Chief, his wife, and his son, that brought tears to my eyes when I watched the news coverage and read reports of gun-toting rebels riding the back of pick-up trucks. When I heard reports of gunfire and machetes, of looting, and rape.

Those villagers of *Zala* do not share many of the privileges in life that I, my family, my neighbors, and my friends have had. But indeed they showed me something we have lost.

Yes, *poor are they in the goods of men,* Kipling said, *but* ever so *rich are they in wonders seen.*

Beauty in the Eyes of the Beholder

Namibia (2002)

Which of us has not been stunned by the beauty
of an animal's skin or its flexibility in motion?

Marianne Moore, *Of Beasts ad Jewels*

I n one thunderous leap he pounced onto the hood of our open
vehicle, landing within just one narrow yard of the veins pulsing
rapidly, very close to my throat. In one liquid movement, he
lowered his head and dug ravenously into the raw flesh before me with
his strong jaw and his ivory-colored teeth. All the while he watched me
intently out of the narrowed corner of his eye. My own jaw fell ajar but
silent at the sight unfolding so close in front of my eyes.

His regal coat was marked with small pools of lustrous black on
heather shades of khaki gold. It was the gold of white sand melted in
honey, the gold of dry sea grass, that of a fine *sauvignon blanc,* of a crisp
white wine. With seductive, penetrating eyes, a sleek head, and smooth,
velvety moves, his suave demeanor was the essence of James Dean; it
was Marlon Brando *cool.* Designed for rapier speed, the cheetah's body
was that of an Olympic champion; he was slender, athletic, and lean.
Perhaps he was a sheer fraction of a minute slower than he should have
been, this handsome carnivore who was missing one front leg. But if so,
it was lost on me, so great were his agility, his strength, and his speed.
We were told his name is *Tyke.*

Tyke and *Spike*. A second cheetah was very close, standing just a foot off the side of the road. Brother and sister, the two made an inseparable feline pair. Now more than ten years old, these cheetahs had been orphaned as infants a decade earlier by the sliding wheels and screeching brakes of a speeding motor vehicle that crushed *Tyke's* leg. The car also claimed their mother in an untimely death, leaving these two cheetahs orphaned, alone. The teardrops staining *Tyke* and *Spike's* cheeks with small rivers of black spoke of the tragedy in their lives and the sorrow of many of their kin. Such is life where man and nature clash in their competing claims for open space. Half a world away from home, I had entered country that once belonged to these stunning animals, these great spotted cats. I could not help myself but marvel as I watched the beauty of these live wonders of the feline world.

Orphaned before they learned to hunt, *Tyke* and *Spike* were at once both doomed and privileged to a pampered and protected life at the cheetah orphanage I was visiting; it was an unintended country club of sorts, a mixed blessing where free food and safety from predators are lifelines without which these two wild animals could not survive. But free food comes at a heavy price. The fee exacted for room service meals delivered each day is the wire fence that limits the distance these spirited racers can run. It is the thin cords of metal that delineate where these wild cats can and cannot roam. Like a deal with the devil, it is the gift that steals the freedom at the center of their hearts even while it protects their hides and proffers their only means to survive. Life without liberty. A seductive but *very* high price to pay.

Today's dinner was delivered on the hood of our Jeep.

I had traveled eighteen long hours in a dull and unremarkable jet from Singapore, from the heat and humidity of the Southeast Asian tropics. I had traded an immaculate city-state where life runs like clockwork and the lawns are a beautifully trimmed bright, velvety, emerald green, for an unparalleled open-air zoo and the oldest, most remarkable desert on earth. A desert whose late afternoon makes orange, gold, brown, and blue a fashion statement of extraordinary sorts. The *Namib*. It is a place where the sun-kissed dunes reach for the clear azure sky with their brilliant coppery-orange curves. Where golden sands rise and curve sensuously like a voluptuous woman lying seductively on her side. It is a place where tiny silica fragments blow with the wind and change color with the sun. Where cobras flare their bronze-colored hoods in a vivid reminder of who really owns this magnificent, if arid, place. In the *Namib*, beauty stretches as far as the eyes can see but pain is real and Nature is harsh. It is a place where the very sun that warms the cold also evaporates the water, and dries the rain. In doing so it steals the moisture that preserves life, even while it nurtures the same.

Namibia is, as my friends who lived there say, *Africa for Beginners*. With its clean streets and modern buildings, *Windhoek*, the capital, provides an easy landing in a continent where chaos is common and urban orderliness is rare. A clean, sparsely populated country where profound poverty exists but infrastructure is good and the daily trappings of life generally work well, Namibia served up a superb vacation for me that, over decades, has been rivaled by few.

We watched as *Tyke* cleaned his plate, or rather the dark green hood of our Jeep. We watched as he consumed every morsel of fresh, sinewy, red meat with purposeful speed. And then in a split-second flash he was gone, just a distant memory in a fleeting moment of time. The ebony spots that float across his coat of gold did not seem a sufficient cover in the thin strands of the dry savannah grass until he disappeared before our eyes, melting into his environment as smoothly as a master magician's trick. In one silent breath of air he vanished, even as we watched where he settled down in the low, dry grass just a few feet away. With an artist's brush strokes, Nature has created camouflage to perfection, making me shudder as I think back ten years to the game park in Uganda where the vehicle I was in during a game park drive became so hopelessly stuck in the mud that we all had to get out of the vehicle and push. Surrounded by shoulder-high grass, with no weapons of any sort, our hearts skipped a collective beat on discovering that within three feet of our minivan were the very fresh paw prints of a lioness and her cubs. Mama and her young could not have been far away as we seven tourists stood offering ourselves up like tasty entrées on the *menu du jour*. Lucky for us the lions must have already dined.

A cheetah like *Tyke* that loses its mother before the age of two years old cannot live in the wild on its own. In the simple rules of feline DNA and the centuries-old order of the animal kingdom, no surrogate can or will teach a young cheetah orphan to successfully execute a hunt, to stalk its prey and make the necessary kill that will fill its stomach and nourish its bones. Yet, hunting, for a cheetah, like any wild carnivore, is his meal ticket. It is the price of his dinner. It is a make-or-break bush life skill. Lacking the skill to stalk and kill its prey, a young orphan becomes nothing more than the tantalizing appetizer to another predator's repast. The pair before me was blessed to have been taken in by *AfriCat Foundation's* Cheetah Orphanage, a non-profit project of high regard and international repute that rescues and rehabilitates injured animals, works with ranchers to find solutions to the commercial tension between the domesticated livestock that now graze the farms and the wild animals who once ruled the land. *AfriCat Foundation* teaches school children the importance of conservation, the value of wild game. They teach the necessity of balance in the ecosystem, and the respect for nature that is so critical to a peaceful coexistence in a land that man has tried with only limited success to claim and commercialize as his own.

The taupe, oat, and bran-colored brush tickled our calves and swiped our knees as we walked over the lumpy, uneven ground. The electronic beep emanating intermittently from the radio tracking device, the swish of dry grass against our legs, the crunch of thorn bushes underfoot, and the wind whispering in our ears were the only sounds as the morning sky stood silent and blue. It was an exceptionally rare invitation my French friend Bernard and I had been given, to track two cheetahs on foot. The orphanage had two adolescents nearly ready to release. In this half-way house of brush and termite mounds and dust, our task for the morning was to find the pair and observe them closely for a moment —

just long enough to discern if they were holding their own or they were losing weight, if they showed signs of injury or ill health that would indicate a less than successful transition back to unassisted bush life. Failure to thrive would preclude a release into the wild where these two cheetahs would once again be fully on their own against the test of nature and predators and man but this pair passed our test. Unlike *Tyke* and *Spike*, these two already knew how to hunt; we had only needed to confirm by observation that they still remembered how.

We had rented a car with a driver and immediately headed north. We were nearly the only ones on the smooth asphalt road. Across miles of barren landscape we drove under a cloudless sky and a rich, warm sun. So lonely was the highway that in fact most traffic accidents involve not two vehicles, but one. The other party to any mishap is usually an antelope, a *Kudu*, or a large cat.

We were a few hours out of *Windhoek* when we saw the first baboons. A hapless, jovial, disorganized welcoming committee, they bounced around like a group of preteens on a school outing or a weekend camping trip. Thirty or more of these hairy animals lined our way. Their drab-colored skin, their hirsute backs, long arms, and awkward, uneven gait said little about my not-so-distant relatives' coordination, cunning, audacity, and speed; appearances can be very deceiving. I recalled a pair of missionaries in West Africa telling me years before of coming home one afternoon to find that a troop of baboons had decided their kitchen was a mighty fine place to play. The primates had made a mess of the pots and pans and took off like bandits with a substantial stash of food, scattering the rest on the kitchen and living room floors. Just a few years later, in Botswana, I would hear similar tales from restaurant staff, of baboons and monkeys raiding the dining rooms, running off faster than the waiters could chase, with the salt shakers, the pepper shakers, and the bread.

Eager to see our first lion, *Wildebeest*, or giraffe as we drove north, our eyes scoured the landscape for anything big that moved. For mile after mile we scanned the flat earth, the dry hills, the massive boulders and the numerous piles of rocks. We searched the scant bushes and scattered trees, looking for some big shadow or some telling silhouette, watching for the slightest of movement behind the cover of brush. But it is amazing the tricks your eyes will play.

It's just a cow, said the driver with a newly-formed smile on his thin lips and a soft chuckle in his voice.

When we got close enough to see, I laughed loudly in embarrassment as I realized it was true. More than once one or another of our party of three mistook a termite mound for an elephant, a bush for a deer, and even a big rock for a giraffe. It all seems so simple from the distance of another country, sitting in a living room and looking at a professional photographer's wildlife pictures in a beautiful coffee table book. Or during a leisurely stroll at the city zoo, where the animals are easy to spot amid the fake boulders and skinny trees of their surrogate habitat. But shadows play games, the mind plays tricks, and wishful thinking comes to bear in those first hours and days in the game parks and animal reserves of this continent wealthy in fauna, rich in wild game.

Alas in just two days in *Etosha* National Park we saw more animals than we could count. We saw vast herds of giraffe with their long legs, willowy necks, gentle stride, and their large, inquisitive eyes. We saw a lion pair on the distant shore of a watering hole where the other animals stood in a state of guarded alert, few daring to bend down for a much-coveted drink. We saw hundreds of *Springbok* and *Gemsbok* and Gazelle. We passed large *Secretary Birds*, and saw Ostrich with their round bodies, long legs, thin necks, and disproportionately small heads. Perhaps a joke by Nature, an Ostrich's eyeball is bigger than its brain.

We saw the camel- and ivory-colored coats of the *Kudu*, something I can imagine Jonathon Adler might create. We saw the Impala's horns, beautifully curved like a ballerina's slow *pirouette*. A Hedgehog ate discarded lettuce, shrouded in the darkness of night. And we watched massive herds of Buffalo thunder across the plains, raising thick clouds of dust to choke the late afternoon sky. We waited patiently numerous times while hundreds of Zebra crossed the road immediately in front of our car. These handsome animals walked with the smooth step of a model and the elegance of a storybook queen. We watched as herds of elephants lumbered into view, bathed in the water holes and powdered their backs with the dry dirt of the late Namibia winter's day.

If Nature is a scientist, she is also an *artiste extraordinaire.* She is a sculptor, a painter, a craftsman, a draftsman, a musician, a choreographer, and a colorist beyond compare. The dark *espresso* stripes of a Zebra's back surpass the skillful brush strokes of a master calligrapher's hand. The mottled brown of the lion's mane eclipses any painter's masterpiece, and the deep resonating sound of a lion's early morning roar puts even the most talented tenors to shame. The sunset that fades to amethyst from orange, and the agate-hued feathers of the vulture speak of an exquisite beauty and refinement only a few rarefied stylists have; perhaps Armani took a color cue from this world for his rich, subdued palettes of sophisticated slate, oatmeal, charcoal, taupe, and steel blue.

The deep crevices that form an adventurous road map on the shadowy leather of the elephant's hide lend a rich texture to the product of the professional photographer's lens. The sweet call of the wild birds dances on the wind. The sharp chorus of alarm that rings out across the sky heralds the predator's approach. What orchestra can match the sounds of the animal kingdom in which the insects, the reptiles, the mammals, and the birds each play their own distinct part? What dance troupe can approach the movement of a herd of antelope as they run in a gentle arc or they dart suddenly to the left, then the right? And what designer would have created a coat of quills, even if of the most beautiful translucent coffee, ebony, and vanilla, as the nocturnal Hedgehog wears? Words cannot adequately describe the scenes that unfolded artistically before our eyes.

With unbridled imagination Nature created patches on the giraffe's back that resemble the map of France; she dressed the leopard with a coat covered by small puddles of ink. What creativity Nature expressed, crowning the lion with his mane, and giving the rhinoceros his horn.

What ingenuity she exercised to give some creatures long legs and others short. To empower some with brute strength and others with the speed of light. To have some creatures meander in the broad light of day, while gifting others to excel under the dark cover of night. But today, the numbers of most big game in Africa are in step decline. Decades of hunting to protect livestock, to collect animal parts, or to practice questionable sport have decimated populations of leopard, cheetah, lion, elephant, rhinoceros, and more. Even as their beauty and power electrify the imagination, so do Africa's animals drive some sad souls to pay as much as $100,000 U.S. just for the right to bag a dubious *trophy* and carry it home.

If Nature put art in the animals and the land, she also blessed the people of the ancient *Namib* and *Kalahari* deserts with an innate artistic flair. It is evidenced by the starbursts, the animals, the spirals, the diamonds, and the waves of rich, warm colors woven into baskets by the skillful fingers and strong hands of Namibia's rural women. Like the hand-made carpets of the Moroccan *bled*, the intertwined reeds and grass tell a powerful story of beauty and hardship and life. And just like the carpets of Morocco whose earthen hues of ochre and indigo and gold are being replaced by violent lavender and shocking pink of the chemists' vials and a maniac's dreams, Namibia's traditional art is surrendering today to a new demand of a modern time. Once the province and product of rural practicality and everyday use, increasingly today's basketry is made for sale to the relatively rich tourists who want not so much an authentic artifact, as a souvenir that fits their faraway living room or bedroom or kitchen décor. Increasingly its designs and motifs are not influenced by the animals and plants of the desert and the local culture and lore, but by designers and marketers in New York and Paris and L.A.

Baskets that were once the brown and beige and henna and gold of nature can now be found in whatever color you need to match your modern life, made creatively from natural materials, synthetic fibers, brightly-colored telephone wire, or recycled plastic bags. Whether this is devaluing tradition and indigenous art or just a clever way of putting a new twist on the old, visitors increasingly want pop culture and contrived commodity design. And as wealthy international consumers vote with their wallets, with their credit cards, and their cash, the women who too often earn less than one thin dollar a day adapt to the universal laws of successful commerce and do what every good business person will do. They make what sells, putting into question the future of time-honored traditional art and design. As in so many other places I visit around the globe, Namibia's culturally authentic art may, in my own lifetime, die. But who am I, blessed with a full stomach, a closet of clothes, and a solid roof over my head, to say forgoing heritage to earn a better living is wrong? And would I, born and raised in the most consumer-oriented society on earth, really want to give up the indulgence of choice in the market place?

While some things change, so do others quietly stand still. Such is the case with Namibia's two-leafed *Welwitschia* plant. A testament to endurance, to survival in one of the best but also one of the most trying of places, these timeless *Welwitschia* live to be over two *thousand* years old. Their rumpled, dusty, drab green leaves fall in a lazy, elongated heap, looking nonetheless, pretty fresh for the centuries they have survived. It was not without amazement that we looked at these living, two-leafed wonders and pondered the changes they, over the millennia, have seen. I tried to imagine the storms they have endured, the droughts they have sustained, the sun they have relished, the animals that have walked by. But even if time stood still for the *Welwitschia*, it moved on unapologetically for us; our days were running short. From *Etosha* we turned around and we continued our travels, this time heading south.

In the gentle hours of the soft, early morning southern Namibia light, the air was quiet and fresh and cool. Standing before us at the silent break of day was a giant raised, harmonic form. Snakelike and smooth, *Dune Number 45* was shaped with precision by the wind and colored by the sun. Finely crafted and serpentine in shape, this august, magnificent wind-crafted pile of sand measures over one thousand feet in height.

169

Standing in the cool air of the night before, we watched as the sun rose that morning, ascending slowly and evenly in the newly awakening sky. In one smooth progression of color and light the sun gradually lit one side of *Dune 45* and its neighbors. As the minutes passed, one side turned from once-gold to a bright, fire-brand orange, brilliant pumpkin, the color of a persimmon ripened by the sun. The back side, in contrast remained dark. It remained hidden, cloaked in a shadow, deprived of the expanding light of day. In those first hours, when the air was still cool, and the day was still fresh, before the sun rose high in the clear blue sky, each dune was colored one side bright and one side dark. Black shadows rested like tar on one side in vivid contrast to the other whose sienna orange was set on fire by the sun that climbed ever higher in the brilliant, cloudless sky. Like *yin* and *yang*, orange and black gave fine definition to the striking *S* that formed the backbone of these captivating, commanding, awe-inspiring Namibian dunes.

When the morning passed and the sun had changed sides, black warmed to gold, to rust, then to a bright mid-day tangerine. In turn, on the other side of *Dune 45's* wind-sharpened ridge of sand, orange slowly faded to gray until the afternoon's setting sun sent a flood of charcoal pouring down this side, now newly hidden from the shifting light of day.

These were the much-photographed dunes of *Sossusvlei*, with their never-ending artistic cycle of alternating light and dark. I beheld them momentarily in silence, for they are the oldest and the tallest dunes found anywhere on earth.

Under the day's mid-morning sun, these majestic mountains of sand first seemed a motionless, lifeless work of art, a painter's three-dimensional still life, a photograph trapped in time. In my assessment, however, I could not have been more wrong. A hike along the razorback that separates sienna from black on imperial *Dune Number 45* revealed an astonishing collection of assorted tracks a tiny fraction of the size of my own. Bearing remarkable witness to nature's strength, courage, persistence, and drive, many thousands of prints wound from here to there, from left to right, newly etched in the pristine canvas of fresh, wind-blown sand. Each trail marked with precision the tedious journey a tiny beetle, a lizard, a rodent, or a snake had made. Offering a brief testimony to the variety of wildlife that call these dunes their home, these trails last only a moment or an hour until a new breath of wind commands the most minute silica particles to scurry one over another, sliding into new positions that obliterate any temporary, short-lived records of the immediate and temporary past. It is an eternal *Sisyphean* dance through space. It is a race against the shifting sands. A horizon forever changing. It is a moment lost forever in time.

We were leaving *Sossusvlei* when my eyes caught a fluid movement in a determined path, traversing the dirt road immediately in front of our car. A rich bronzy-black patina, like that of tarnished but lovingly well-worn silver flashed in the bright sunlight of the mid-day. A cobra caught my eye as he slipped smoothly from our left to our right as if gliding over a polished sheet of glass; his slender body covered twelve or fifteen feet in the time I could take just a short breath or two. And then as we stopped our vehicle, he stopped; he seemed to know I wanted a closer, more intimate look. Just as I looked down from my window, he looked up at me. It took him only a fraction of a second to raise his head a foot off the hardened, gravel-strewn road and spread his lustrous hood. I had seen cobras in the wild before, but always from a comfortable distance as they raced over folded, dried grass to get hastily away from me. This was the first one out of captivity that I had seen up close; it was the first cobra out of captivity that I had seen spread his hood. I recalled a postcard I had received as a child, with a commanding picture of a King Cobra, his hood spread wide. I was reminded, once again, as with the cheetahs, the leopard, the zebras, the elephants, and the giraffes, of the beauty, the magnificence, and the mystique of the animals to which this southern Africa land really belongs.

Hours later in that same arid mid-October day, we had exchanged the *Namib's* smooth waves of burnt orange for a dry and mottled gray of another desert. We now stood amidst the beige and brown and taupe of the *Kalahari*. We had traveled further to the south and it was late in the afternoon. Standing tall in an open expanse I gazed over the land that lay before and around me. Our trip was coming to an end; I contemplated the beauty I had seen, the grace and the power I had witnessed. I considered the lives of the animals and the people and their difference from mine. I thought about my travels and my destinations and the footprints I invariably leave behind. A late afternoon breeze picked up, blowing nearly invisible bits of grit and sand. As the wind blew in my face, I felt as if I were being admonished by a thousand stinging arrows of conscience and wind-driven sand for I tread on a sacred place, a heaven-like place on earth, a holy place. So easy is it to get caught up, as a traveler, in the adventure and the romance of a trip like this and to forget the sanctity of nature and the gift of our time in its midst.

As I watched the sun sink slowly from the early evening sky, a blanket of darkness settled gently around me and a great chorus of stars emerged to sing its lullaby to me there on the edge of the *Kalahari*. As I stood in the near silence of the resplendent and distant place that had so gifted me with beauty, my conscience questioned the ease with which I touched this tiny corner of the seemingly otherwise untouched earth. I reflected on the flora and the fauna. I thought about the desert and the acacia trees and the waterholes and the animals. In my mind I revisited the Namibian bush. In those moments in the fading sun, the wind and the sand, cut like tiny daggers of glass, conspiring to remind me that I stood on hallowed ground.

Soon I heeded the brisk reminder and I retreated to the lodge for a lovely glass of fine South African white wine.

In Namibia, as nowhere before, I was gifted with the vast beauty of nature. I was gifted with the boundless elegance and the power of Africa's big game. Gifted with the gazelle's dance and the elephant's lumbering walk. I was gifted with the cheetah's coat of black on gold. Gifted with the show of a cobra regally spreading his lustrous bronze-black hood and I was gifted with the calligraphy of the Zebra's coat. I was witness to the courage and endurance of the oldest living plants on earth.

In Namibia, unlike almost anywhere I'd been before, I was gifted by Nature, extraordinarily so. I was awestruck by the simplicity and texture of the elephant's hide, by the Zebra's stripes, the lion's roar, and by the hedgehog's coat of quills. By the plants and the animals, and the sun on the shifting sands. In the words of Marianne Moore, I was *stunned by the beauty of an animal's skin.* I was mesmerized by *Nature's flexibility in motion.* I was captivated by the cheetah's leap and the cobra's glide. I was humbled. I was amazed. I was quieted. I was awed. I was gifted in Namibia with sights and scenes and reflection that I cannot, that I will not, that I must not easily forget.

Nine Year Olds Picking Your Beans

El Salvador (2006)

Conscience.
A personal sense of the moral content of one's own conduct, intentions, or character
with regard to a feeling of obligation to do right or good.

Encyclopædia BRITANNICA online

on't take the buses.
Don't walk alone and don't go to the parks.
El Salvador?
*You're going **where**?*
Don't travel there by yourself.

It was January 2006. Three weeks earlier I had joined the flood of foreigners who travel past the security walls, the barbed wire, and the armed guards of Guatemala City to the fifty-some language schools operating in *Antigua*, Guatemala. It is just one of the many cities and towns across Mexico, Central, and South America that sell Spanish lessons to an unending torrent of university students, backpackers, consultants, housewives, vacationers, and retirees seeking something more authentic for their recreational time than package tours and fun-in-the-sun.

For more than a fortnight beautiful Antigua wrapped me in its folds as energetic young Guatemalan language instructors pelted me with verb tenses and vocabulary. For three weeks this charming old colonial town had held me in its warm embrace with its festive colors, lacy wrought iron window grates, smooth cobblestones, and flowering potted plants. It captivated me with its wedding cake churches and its magnificently restored convents, its warm days and its cold nights. With the incessant earsplitting pops and bangs of firecrackers twenty-four hours a day. It entertained me with its art galleries, music concerts, coffee shops, and Internet cafés. Its salsa lessons, its volcanoes, and its animated Central Park.

But amid the beauty and brilliant colors of the hand-woven Guatemalan cloth something was missing. Between the thunderous drumming and the lively notes of the visiting musicians from Havana's *Buena Vista Social Club* there was a noticeable void. Amid the deep, rich aroma of freshly brewed coffee. Against the sweetly familiar and unexpectedly foreign flavor of hot chocolate with an enticing Latin American cinnamon twist. Over the backdrop of blue skies and forested hills, and in the gray ash-filled smoke spiraling upwards from a volcano on the edge of town, there was something that was absent, there was something that was just not there.

In spite of visits to the nearby pueblos by brightly painted *chicken bus* and a rusted pick-up truck whose creases and dents give testimony to a full life and a hard road. In spite of the dark eyes, warm smiles, friendly ways, and honey-colored skin of the Guatemalan people. Amid the weekend tours to the ancient jungle-cloaked Mayan pyramids of *Tikal*, and a trip to *Todo Santos* with its spirited men in their straw hats and red striped pants. Between *pretérito* and *presente*, *hijos* and *hijas*, verb tenses and vocabulary. Amid, between, against all that, something was missing for me.

What are you doing next week?
I'm traveling to El Salvador, I said.
*You're going **where**? And **why**?*
*And **how**?*
I was going by public bus.

178

For one hundred-twenty *quetzales* I bought a one-way bus ticket and headed south.

Four hours later, after smoothly paved roads in a comfortable and modern coach, I exchanged the dulled barbed wire of Guatemala City for shiny concertina razor wire that glistens in the sun, sitting loopity-loop in big circles atop the security walls, roof tops, and gates in *San Salvador*. I traded in the sight of the colorful post-colonial ethnic dress of Guatemala's indigenous children, women, and men for El Salvador's generic Western clothes. I replaced the well-worn *quetzales* in my wallet for wrinkled green dollars, the currency of my own home. And I left warm weather for hot.

Some travel books and websites say the best reason to visit El Salvador is that no one else does. It was not so far from the truth. Only after I arrived did I begin to fully appreciate how strikingly few travelers ventured across the border to visit this small volcano-studded patch of land.

Facing the great Pacific Ocean, El Salvador boasts sport fishing, surfing, and three hundred kilometers of beautiful beach. With upwards of seventy-five volcanoes, if you count the young and the old, this eight-thousand square-mile piece of geography offers an interesting landscape with humps and bumps and mountains and hills that occasionally smoke, rumble, and roar as the *Santa Ana* volcano did just a few weeks before I arrived. With *pupusas, licuados*, shrimp, fresh fish, and *married rice and beans*, El Salvador serves up a flavorful, filling, and inexpensive cuisine. Its landscape is dressed with abundant flowers in every color known to man. With birds in rich ruby, turquoise, emerald, and amber jewel-toned plumes, the colors of precious and semiprecious stones, El Salvador offers eye candy like nowhere else. The faded glory and muted rose, coral, olive, and beige of a hand-painted ceiling in a two-hundred-year old church offered peace and a gentle sense of calm as the soft notes of an acoustic guitar floated through the warm, mid-day air. They were released to the winds by the gentle fingers of an old man with grayed hair, soft, dark eyes, and deep furrows in his tanned and tired face. And the country's unique *Pipil* and Mayan sites, if not as grand as the Mayan remnants in its neighbors to the north, still make an archaeology enthusiast's eyes light and feet dance.

In El Salvador's crowded markets where the artist's palette is not acrylics and oils but the fruits, vegetables, and flowers of a fertile volcanic ground, I longed for my kitchen as I walked between baskets of red chilies, purple onions, and a wide variety of squash sitting choc-a-bloc between bags of rice and sacks of beans. Next to piles of bananas, boxes of melons, crates of red tomatoes. Behind bunches of fresh cilantro with its crisp, fragrant smell, colorful oranges, bell peppers, cabbage, and greens. I longed to have one of the women in the market teach me her own recipes for the produce she peddled at mere pennies to the pound.

The travel books were right; notably few tourists visit El Salvador. I was one of only two foreigners on the filled-to-capacity, fifty-six seat bus going south from Guatemala City to *San Salvador*. And I was the only one without Central American blood. A bit like traveling in Asia during the *SARS* epidemic, I was one of only three or four foreigners in a big *San Salvador* hotel. I was one of four travelers seeking day tours from the capital. Joined by an Italian, a British woman, and a Pole we formed our own little United Nations of tourism, and we had the country largely to ourselves.

I wanted nothing more than to experience El Salvador not from the outside but from within. Not just to pass the *maquilladoras* that make so many American clothes, where the workers were newly hopeful for the benefits of *CAFTA*, while leery that the advantages of this free-trade agreement would be a one-way street.

I wanted not just to see homes from the outside. Not just to see the bullet holes that still marred the exterior of so many houses left from the all-too-recent civil war, but to talk with the people who live inside. Not just to watch the hills roll by, but to climb their wooded slopes. When I felt three tremors in two days, I wanted to *see* the gods of fire at the *Santa Ana* volcano roar, not just hear about them on the evening news.

I had really wanted to backpack around the country on my own. I had really wanted to ride the local buses from town to town and to stay in small *posadas* and local hotels. But those more thoughtful and more experienced than me say wisdom is the better part of valor. Eventually I capitulated to what the locals told me, skipping the do-it-alone-by-bus routine in favor of a private vehicle and a local guide. Hard to tell whether it was really a class-related ego issue or an appropriate safety call, but one *Salvadoreño* after another told me no middle class nationals would ride a local bus. When I asked what sort of difficulties or dangers they thought I, a foreign woman taking the buses alone might face, each one queried gave me the same response. Wide eyes. Raised eyebrows. And a look that asked if I were *loca*. Had I gone mad?

I had not gone mad. I merely wanted, really wanted, simply wanted to experience El Salvador somewhat like the locals do. As much, at least, as I could with my English tongue, my fair skin, my *gringa* wardrobe, and my North American ways. I did not want to repeat my last China experience of being shuttled from one fancy hotel to another in the comfort and sterility of a private car, while my backpack and hiking boots rode unused in the back.

The gangs, they all said.
The problem on the buses is the gangs.
What about the gangs? I asked.

Those more knowledgeable than me said the gangs rode the buses to rob those passengers just trying to get from *point A* to *point B* in their ordinary daily routine.

It doesn't happen all the time and it happens much less now than before. But it is still a risk you should not take, they said.

Who would think people would declare it unsafe for me to ride the buses in a place three countries away from my own because of the ways and the crimes and the lifestyles of the young men and women in the cities and the states of the country I left behind? It is sometimes surprising to me the way things are geopolitically intertwined. Who would have thought the neighborhoods of Los Angeles would shape my vacation plans in a different part of the globe? But they did. As I embarked on my El Salvador trek, I learned another piece in the world puzzle of politics, migration, and crime.

I learned that the gang violence of this Central American country is not simply a home-grown ill. It is instead, at least in part, a link in an international chain of events that binds two seemingly unrelated countries in an unfortunate and circular way. El Salvador may have produced the ingredients for this crime-driven violence, but my own country added the spice.

In the 1980s, El Salvador's wide disparity in economic opportunity and wealth erupted in a devastating and bloody civil war. When bullets riddled houses and airplanes bombed churches many nationals sought and found refuge and refugee status in El Salvador's big brother to the north. In my homeland, in *los Estados Unidos,* the United States. They moved into the cities and the *barrios,* the neighborhoods, and the slums of what many consider the greatest modern-day nation on earth.

But somewhere north of the border good intentions and humanitarian plans collided head-on with the cold reality of living as a refugee in a foreign land. Many who sought a safe haven in the land of opportunity instead found a country whose official language they did not understand. They found a school system already overloaded and overstressed. They found they could ill afford the goods in the market. They found laws that say who can work and who cannot. They found the intense pressures of an economy that while more egalitarian than their own, still favors higher education, that most often rewards the already-rich, and often overlooks the marginalized poor. They found a land that outlaws racism and ethnic discrimination but where it sadly still exists.

The vast majority of Salvadorians are good, hard-working people with strong values and a clear sense of right and wrong. But the cold reality of life as a refugee claimed a few victims of its own. Too many of those same young boys who with their families fled El Salvador's civil war fell through the United States of America's socioeconomic and educational cracks. Instead of finding safety and success, instead of realizing the *Great American Dream*, a fraction of those transplants migrated into the gun shops, tattoo parlors, and violent ways of the inner city gangs. They unsuspectingly left the bullets and machetes and bombs of El Salvador for the guns and gangs of the streets of Los Angeles. Instead of building a life of safety and success, too many of the young immigrant boys and men slipped into the seductive life of gang violence and crime.

When the U.S. Government enhanced its efforts to thwart terrorism and reduce crime, those immigrants who had not played by the rules were justifiably shipped back home for the crimes they committed in the United States. But they did not travel lightly on their journey back south. They did not travel unaccompanied. They did not travel alone.

Along with the clothes on their backs and the tattoos on their arms, these young men carried home their new-found, violent ways. Their suitcases carried not just clothes and a toothbrush and a comb; they also carried the habits and the attitudes of the gangs of Los Angeles; their knapsacks carried the violent rules of the North American inner city streets. Once back in the land of their birth, the emigrants-come-home reportedly terrorized the buses of El Salvador instead of the streets of East L.A. Little did anyone think ten years before that a shadow of El Salvador's civil war would once again be revisited on the people of this fertile country and beautiful land in a vicious cycle and an unfortunate *karma* of what goes around comes around. The young boys of El Salvador fled bullets and firearms and violence only to carry them back home.

Don't travel by bus, the *Salvadoreños* I asked unanimously said.

And so after arriving in *San Salvador*, I traveled with a local guide in a private van. With four wheels and a few tanks of gas we traced the outline of a splendid clover leaf. Down and up. Around and around. We drove to the Pacific coast with its blue water, white waves, and black sand. We circled volcanoes. We looked at natural beauty, ancient architecture, and mangrove swamps. We rounded forested hills, we passed bare rocks, and thirty-year old lava flows.

And we passed the greatest variety of green foliage I have ever seen. Every shape and shade and texture imaginable. We passed short banana trees and tall, slender pines. Cactus and ferns and philodendron. Feathered palms whispering secrets to the wind, and bamboo shooting to the sky. We stood under the cooling shade of a giant mango tree, and we studied the forked leaves of papaya trees reaching for the clouds. We passed dagger-like Yucca plants and waxy Rubber Trees. We walked under cashew trees with their broad leaves and pear-shaped fruit.

We passed vast fields where the orange-yellow flames of efficiency and ease licked the stalks of the sugarcane, as slash-and-burn agriculture scorched the earth. Villagers with empty kerosene cans waited by the side of the road. In time they would harvest what the fires left behind. My mind raced to newscasts of the out-of-control wildfires back home in Texas. They had just destroyed hundreds of acres and numerous homes, the winds fueling their hunger for yet more land to burn. We passed corn in the fields and birds in the sky. We traversed the lands where jaguars and pumas once roamed. We moved under motionless trees where Spider Monkeys once played. We passed men on horses and women on foot.

And we saw a multitude of flowering plants. We witnessed brilliant yellow blooms dancing across the bare branches of the *Cortez Blanco* tree, bringing a million drops of sunshine to the hills. We passed Christmas-red Poinsettias growing wild along the roads, dotting the landscape like so many scattered pools of blood. We passed violet-colored orchids clinging to the trunks of the host trees they call home, and we passed tangerine-colored flowers waltzing across the field. We saw dark green, burgundy, and bright pink *Coleus* growing like weeds. I smelled the sweet fragrance of white gardenias. I felt the paper-thin *Bougainvillea* blossoms in orange, purple, white, fuchsia, and rose. Tiny yellow flowers no larger than the wings of a fly peppered the ground in front of my feet, and pale lavender-white blossoms larger than my fist graced the branches of a large bush. I saw the red and yellow Hibiscus of my late grandmother's south Florida yard. And the electric pink of the *Impatiens* plant. I saw the neon periwinkle blue of flowers in the cloud forest, against a backdrop of deep, dark green. This Salvadorian scenery was alive with splashes and dots and swipes of the warm colors of a Caribbean artist or a mammoth watercolor set.

As I walked the grounds of *Joya de Cerén*, Central America's own *Pompeii*, I marveled at the centuries-old painted pottery and decorated urns the archaeologists found remarkably well-preserved under multiple meters of thick volcanic ash. Stylized birds and bold geometrics in reds, rusts, black, and brown covered the glazed and polished clay at this solitary *Pipil* site.

As I gazed at the remnants of lava-covered cornstalk-and-mud-packed walls from around 600 A.D., I flashed back to the same construction techniques I had seen thirty minutes before in several of the contemporary rural homes we had passed en route to this archaeology site. Over more than a millennia, very little had really changed.

As I pondered the ancient, unearthed shells of the vacated homes that some of El Salvador's earliest people fled as the earth's ravenous orange tongue rolled down in a molten lava flow, I could see in my mind the televised news reports of residents fleeing the Gulf Coast of the United States when monster hurricanes moved into their towns, unwelcome guests in a land developer's gamble with nature and an unfortunate point in weather and time. In their own unlucky way, those in the U.S. followed the same historic path of others many, many generations before. They unknowingly followed in the footsteps of a people farther south that did not have *FEMA*, the Red Cross, or Habitat for Humanity to help.

El Salvador may not get many visitors but it holds generous rewards for those who go. The people were warm and friendly, with quick smiles.

The vast array of flowers was a feast for even my jaded eyes. And where else can you see multiple volcanoes almost anywhere you turn? Where else can you see such beauty without feeling like one more ant on the tourist picnic of life? In how many places you visit can you see the postcard-perfect view of *Santa Ana's* symmetrical cone before a cloud slips in front to block your view? Where else can you see not just the thrones of the rulers and the temples to the gods of an ancient people, but the habitats and habits of the ordinary citizens' daily lives fourteen hundred years before? Visiting *Joya de Cerén* was a bit like a slice from a unique historical reality program on TV.

As we climbed higher on the paved, serpentine road the air changed from warm to a light, feathery cool. As the foliage grew dense the sunlight overhead danced around us with small bits and pieces of brightness and warmth in a game of *Hide and Seek*. As we rounded each bend, nature presented a new color, a new flower, or a new feathered bird. As we climbed higher, the sweet-sour smell of the fermenting coffee bean pulp tickled my nose as it fertilized the nearby crops. As we continued onward our path rewarded us with glimpses of villagers' everyday routine. Women scrubbed the family clothes in the community basin by the side of the mountain road. Some carried the laundry two miles or more for water to do their wash. Young girls climbed the hills with heavy jugs on their heads, carrying home the necessity of life their own houses do not provide. An old man with gray hair and a tanned and weathered face sat on a big rock, a well-used machete by his side. He was waiting for life, not our van, to pass. A young, barefoot boy with short dark hair and baggy blue pants darted out from behind his house. He was followed by the family's raggedy, copper-haired dog. As we passed the old hand-me-down American school bus with its new coat of bright-colored paint, its stylized acrylic flowers and flames and stripes, I mourned my decision to play it safe, and I wondered whether there were, in fact, any gang members aboard.

As we neared the mountain summits with their stunning, world-class views, we passed the high walls and wire and gates of the land barons' homes. My guide talked of the privilege and power that wealth invariably, in a self-perpetuating, circular fashion, brings. But I did not see the freedom and happiness one might expect of the riches these homes represent. Instead, I saw that each person here, whether rich or poor, lives in his own incarceration of sorts.

More than one-third of the country lives in the unforgiving prison of poverty, earning less than a dollar a day. Most others earn little more. And the remaining few at the top of the economic ladder of success? They, too, live in their own economic jail. It is one of relative or even exorbitant wealth. And those at the summit are the biggest prisoners of their own success. Surrounded by security walls, armed guards, and razor wire, they live too fearful to take the buses, to go to the markets and the parks; they reportedly are afraid to go out, even in their own vehicles, at night.

It was mid-afternoon when we stopped at the vast coffee farm. A well-known *finca* that reportedly supplies some of North America's biggest supermarkets and caffeinated beverage chains. The light mist of the low clouds cooled my shoulders and wet my face as we walked down the cobblestone road between row upon row of coffee bushes and their tall shade trees. I could hear the soft padding of solid feet over the hidden ground in the shadows to my left and my right. I could hear the occasional light chatter of a woman's voice. I could see one man exit the thick wall of hunter green, a one-hundred-twenty-pound sack of beans slung over his hunched shoulders, his head bent down. And I could hear the occasional sing-song words of a young girl or boy. In this age of global consumer awareness and international media pressure they are probably just young children accompanying their parents for lack of a babysitter, a stay-at-home grandparent, or an older sibling, I thought silently to myself. With guarded hope.

Amid the coffee bushes that fill my *lattés* and drain my wallet, I found the sweet smell of rich red beans. I found gentle smiles, warm faces, honest people. I found strong people who work back-breakingly hard. And I found heartache, too.

I watched in silence as the workers exited the coffee orchards at the end of the day. I watched as the branches parted and the workers slipped through the heavy curtains of green. I watched as men and women poured forth, young and old. And I watched as the children came out into the open. Not just one. Not just two. Not just three or four. *But twenty or twenty-five in a total group of about eighty-five.*

Margarita, with her sparkling eyes of coal told me she was nine years old, when I asked her age. Her brother said he was twelve. Both struggled with heavy sacks nearly a third the size of those of the adult men.

In these children I saw the local school house and the empty seats which should have been filled by *Margarita* and her brother *Miguel.* I saw history repeating itself as yet one more young girl and boy would be able to do no better for their own children, because growing up in the prison of poverty they could not get the education they need to do better in their own lives than their impoverished parents have been able to do, in theirs.

I asked *Margarita* what she would do when the coffee beans had all been picked, hoping she would then be going to school.

They would go to pick the next crops, her brother replied, whatever or wherever those commodities might be.

And then I saw another little girl, this one no more than four. She, too, came out from the shadows of the coffee plants with her parents. At only three or four, she already carried her own little basket of beans.

Child labor among the desperately poor is a difficult issue with no easy answer, no fast solution despite what the well-intentioned may believe. El Salvador is not alone. Developing World parents do not want their children, in poverty, to work anymore than my own did, in their relative comfort and wealth. If given a realistic opportunity, these parents would much rather their children receive an education and find better work than the crushing labor they themselves must do. I know these parents do not wish for their own children the hard life they have had. But I also know they find little choice in a place where wages are so low, and prices relatively so high, that it takes all hands on board to feed even a family of four. *Margarita* and *Miguel* work out of necessity, not out of greed. At least not their parents' or their own.

In the determined stride of the women and men exiting the coffee orchards I saw a treadmill of poverty from which they will not likely escape. In the footsteps of those children I saw the untapped potential of El Salvador, my not-so-distant neighbor to the south. In those bulging sacks of dark red beans, I saw not just the freshly brewed coffee or a frothy *latté* drink. I also saw the deeply curved collar bones of *Arturo*, an American acquaintance who grew up in the mountains of Mexico and carried such heavy loads of sugarcane as a child his adult skeleton is permanently deformed.

In the clearing at the edge of those coffee orchards, by the side of the dirt and cobblestone road, I heard the deafening silence of a crowd too tired to talk. I heard the mechanical clacking of the counter weights flying across the slide of a large industrial scale. In one swift motion the weights were propelled across the balance with an efficiency that spoke of a certain boredom with the routine task at hand. The workers gathered round a tall man with black-rimmed eyeglasses, a tattered notebook, and a pen. One at a time, men and women loaded their sacks on the big slab of dark gray steel. As names and numbers filled the notebook, I wondered how many of those being recorded could read a scale and the notations that would ultimately determine their pay at the end of two weeks. I could also not help but wonder if the sacks reportedly weighed as heavy for the accountants when the world commodity price of coffee is low.

But if I found hardship, I also found hope. In El Salvador I found a country that has made great efforts to move beyond its difficult past. I saw evidence of a government that has worked hard to diversify its economy, to build good roads and to propose a new port. I heard of a government that is trying hard to increase tourism and to reduce crime.

189

I found signs of success. I found friendly people and a beautiful land. I found a country not to be overlooked.

And just as I saw the beauty of El Salvador. Just as I learned the things the government is doing right. Just as I learned one more way the geopolitics of different countries is intertwined, just as I learned that this country has much to offer the tourist and the world, I learned one more lesson that sunny afternoon. I learned something in the parade I witnessed, of children, women, and men who exited the coffee groves. I learned something in the engaging eyes, warm smile, and small frame of my namesake *Margarita*, that little Salvadorian girl.

I learned the importance of accepting supermarket prices that allow producers a living wage, that allow parents to educate their kids. That allow fathers and mothers to send their children to school rather than taking them to work in the fields that fill our coffee houses and our supermarket shelves. I learned the importance of buying commodities and crafts from companies with good values and fair practices. I saw the importance of consuming with a conscience. *Of buying Fair Trade.*

A Prism of Ice and Snow

Antarctica (1998)

Who could say what this was, really?

Barry Lopez, *Arctic Dreams and Desire
in a Northern Landscape*

The sky was crystal clear and devoid of sound. The water was a flat sheet of liquid glass. The world was still, almost as if it were not really there. I could have been standing in a photograph, surrounded by nothing but silent nature as I stood on a floor of frigid, gray-green steel. It was close to midnight but time meant nothing and night did not exist in a land where twenty-four hours come and go with no veil of darkness to mark the passing day. I stood in the quiet distance between space and time, alone with just my thoughts, feeling only the magnitude of the splendor that met my eyes and the cold air that kissed my face. To my right were mountains of translucent ice and stacks of virgin snow. To my left was the distant silhouette of an iceberg's tip floating on the horizon that was a distant blue-gray line. Above me was only sunlight and thin air the color of a Robin's egg. There was not a cloud in the sky. No noise touched my ears. No motion tickled the air. Not a ripple moved the water, even as we slipped forward through the clarity of a diamond and the crystalline cold of an Antarctic summer day. This was the trip of my childhood dreams. This was the crown jewel of my travels. This was the dream most people do not even have. In the unforeseen opportunity that came with the end of the *Cold War*, I followed the trail of some of history's greatest explorers, some of the most courageous *voyageurs* of all.

Just days before the smooth water of *Paradise Bay*, the horizon had stood at forty-five degrees to the deck of the Russian spy ship that was my temporary, new-found home. What should have been level was instead standing as cockeyed as the angled pages in the crack of a newly opened book. But the horizon stood to the right for only a moment before the water that buoyed us fell away and the horizon tipped to the left. For a day and a half we rocked and rolled and dipped and lurched through the roughest seas on earth. Through the *Drake Passage*, the ring of water that circles the bottom of the world like a dog chasing its tail. We passed between the wrath of two quarreling typhoons, pitching forward and bouncing back through waters that more than once sent our lunch and dinner dishes careening down the table as if they were hockey pucks on a smooth sheet of ice. One particularly memorable wave propelled our dinner down the table to a fast, ear-splitting crash on the dining room floor. Little did I imagine that night that one day I would see the seas flat as a sheet of glass, reflecting a mirror-perfect image of everything around.

None too soon a geyser of water and the flip of a great forked tail heralded our arrival to the Antarctic Peninsula as a Humpback whale moved in to welcome our boat. I wonder how many times this ambassador in his smooth coat of charcoal gray stepped into this unexpected diplomatic role. Our new escort accompanied us for ten minutes, swimming right by our side as we moved closer to this most mysterious land on earth, its secrets locked in a frozen place and time.

This whale, free to tease the spirits with its jet of white spray and free to feel the cool waters on his smooth, rounded back, was more fortunate than the late owner of the mammoth sun-bleached bones I would see on the pebble-covered shore just a bit later in the week. It is estimated that during the industry's peak, commercial whalers killed as

194

many as forty thousand of these mammals a year, moving from one species of whale to the next, decimating each population in turn and eventually inciting international cries for a stop to the trade. Some nations' fishermen, though, still persist with their hunting and sport even today. And for what? Recent media reports said there was a glut of whale meat on the market in Japan, where young people lack the acquired taste to drive sales to match the aggression of the whalers in this distant sea.

I had waited a long time to make this trip. This was decades after my decision at roughly nine years old to set foot on every one of the seven continents spanning the globe. This was years after the crumbling of the Berlin Wall that turned this Russian spy ship into a rebel without a cause, prompting it to reinvent itself in a mid-life career change from sonar research vessel to tourist boat. But it was years before the National Geographic's *March of the Penguins* showed the world the captivating beauty of the driest and coldest continent on the planet through riveting cinematography, symphony, and tales of avian romance.

Antarctica was a multitude of colors, nearly all of them blue and white. It was white, pearl-like drops dancing on the ridges and tips of the indigo-colored waves. It was the clear blue sky and the thick white fog. It was white, pure white. It was opaque. It was translucent. It was frosted. It was clear. It was easy to understand how the *Inuit* in the far north of the opposite hemisphere could reputedly have countless words for snow. It was white tinged with an ultra sheer wash of ethereal, very pale blue. It was white with the fine blue shadows of the fragile microscopic architecture that makes each snowflake unique. It was a cool blue emanating from within. It was the water reflecting turquoise on the blocks and towers of ice and snow that rise up into the sky like huge crystalline pillars of very light sapphire or quartz.

Though there were occasional interruptions of this two-hue world by rarefied spots of red or orange or brown, they were notably very few.

There were the black rubber *Zodiacs* that carried us from ship to shore. There was the glossy black of our expedition boots, hosed down before and after each trip to land so we carried no contamination from one area to the next. There was the India ink tuxedo on the penguins' shoulders, wings, and back. The fire engine red and the safety orange of our winter parkas deliberately stood out against the Antarctic snow. And the heather brown of a sea lion bull, weighing in at more than two thousand pounds of muscle, bone, and fat lay like a giant slug on the powdery white snow. But in this truncated color spectrum of blue and winter white there was no purple. No pink. No yellow. And a conspicuous absence of green.

There is not *one* picture of the Antarctic beauty, I learned. There is not *one* photograph, *one* video, *one* visual memory that is the same as the next. There were no two days the scenery matched. There were quiet beaches and there was penguin-covered snow. There was empty water as far as the eye could see. There was a horizon broken only by the Polish research station's nearby ship. There was a sea filled with chunks and bits of ragged white, floating about like broken Styrofoam strewn across the kitchen's linoleum floor. There was none of the tourist boredom that eventually sets in when every temple or mountain or market begins to look the same.

There were free-floating icebergs that could be a metaphor for the countries where I travel, I live, and I work, baring only a small fraction of themselves, even to the outsider who observes with a well-trained eye.

There were steep walls of glacial ice and mountains of rock and snow. There were flat, pebble-crusted beaches and places where the snow slipped right into the sea. There were the ice castles of a fairy. There were pristine stretches of frozen land. And there were the rusted carcasses of the machinery, the moth-eaten barrels, and the dilapidated sheds left by legions of whalers who departed or perished decades before, leaving their unsightly mark as a blight on nature and the magnificence of this little-touched paradise where few men and fewer women have stood. There were penguin-covered stretches and scree-covered slopes. There was quiet, motionless beauty, as still as a snapshot in time. And there was the deafening crash of an iceberg calving, dropping its offspring into the frigid waters of the hungry, dark blue sea.

My wonder at the grandeur of Antarctica and the scenery of the Southern Ocean was tempered only by the knowledge that we had to once again cross the untamed waters of the *Drake Passage* where the currents fume, battle, and rage, in order to get back home.

With the intoxicating mixture of excitement and trepidation that schoolchildren feel lining up for a Disneyland ride we climbed tentatively one at a time down the steps that hugged the ship's tall, steep side for our much-anticipated trips to the Antarctic shore. Boarding the small rubber *Zodiacs* in privileged groups of four to six, we stepped wide into the bobbing dinghies to avoid a paralyzingly cold bath that greeted us all around.

It was only once we were set adrift from our giant mother of painted iron and steel that we really understood just what very small and vulnerable fish we were in a very big and fickle sea. Just one quick, unexpected, vanquishing descent of thick gray-white fog, one strong gust of well-placed wind, or one hungry lap of the sea's tongue is all it would have taken to separate us from the ship and the life, the family, and friends we once knew. For all its beauty and its tranquility, Antarctica is a place that does not easily forgive an error, does not easily forget a miscalculation, does not easily overlook an oversight or a human mistake. It is a place where weather conditions can change dramatically in the blink of an eye. Sunny and clear one minute, socked in with a thick curtain of heavy fog the next. Still air one moment, gusts with the force of a speeding train just a breath away. In this temperamental environment of mercurial deities, the slightest misstep, the smallest error in judgment can quickly cost you your life. Though we stripped down to thin t-shirts at times, our thermal jackets and thick parkas were never far away as we stood in the province of the unpredictable and capricious whims of the polar gods, for Antarctica is a land of sudden and tempestuous change.

For good reason Antarctica is called by many a land of extremes. The temperatures can plummet to a bone-jarring eighty-nine degrees below zero, Centigrade. *Minus one hundred twenty-nine* on the Fahrenheit scale. That is before calculating the wind chill that drives the effective temperature much further down. But it can also soar to a relatively balmy sixty degrees Fahrenheit, in round numbers. Winds can reach three hundred kilometers an hour. The *Kabatic Winds*, they are called, christened with their very own name. Or the air can stand perfectly still. The sun never sleeps, or it hides all day, for weeks and months on end. And in some places the ice is three miles thick. Antarctica has never had an indigenous population of its own, yet it magnetically attracts individuals from every corner of the globe. It is the only continent to have never experienced war on its soil. It is for some the ultimate environment for scientific research. For others the apex of a lifetime of travel. It is also, many believe, the bellwether of global warming, with a foreboding tale to tell.

The disintegration of a Rhode Island-sized piece of ice in 2002 greatly alarmed scientists who study these things. In the fifty years following the end of the Second World War, Antarctica reportedly experienced warming at *five* times the average for the globe. Seven ice shelves lost more than *seventeen thousand* square kilometers in the first thirty years after 1974. The *Adele* penguin population has declined by a third, owing, it is believed, to the reduction in the size of the ice shelf it calls its home. If these are the harbingers of climate change as many knowledgeable scientists claim, we may be seeing just the proverbial tip of the Antarctic iceberg of what is yet to come as the oceans warm and life within and around succumbs to a new world order whose consequences we have not yet seen.

We were an interesting assortment of people aboard the recycled, retooled, reinvented boat. *Heinz 57 Varieties* had nothing on us. We included a Russian Captain. We included a Russian and Canadian crew. There were business people. There was a travel writer in our party. Bureaucrats, scientists, students, and a teacher or two. An air traffic controller was aboard, and a retired *WAC*. A couple in their eighties so frail that only with great difficulty could they make it up and down the stairs or around the boat. A carefree twenty-something pair backpacking down the long South American coast belonged to our group. But more than any tour group I have encountered in any other place, we were an extraordinarily well-traveled gaggle of geese. Few countries the world over had not seen one or another of our wayfaring troop.

Our ship, too, was a well-traveled sea-faring craft. Far from its original home in the frozen Russian North, it was a fine example of the new-found friendships and heady business deals that followed the collapse of the Soviet Union and the much-trumpeted end of the *Cold War*. In an ironic twist of politics and time, this reinvented vessel was now carrying the well-paying citizens of the capitalist countries on which it once spied. But outfitted with extra stabilizers to ensure the capture of good data by its scientific listening machines, our craft made for a much smoother ride than we otherwise would have had, despite those days our dinner plates took flight. The reinvented progeny of a new republic, this boat that was once the child of Soviet dreams and Communist ways now benefited from fat wallets fed by profit-driven commercial success and the freedom to travel that democracy allows.

This Russian Connection played out in other small and unexpected ways aboard the *Akademic Ioffe*. On vacation from the steppes of Central Asia it was me, not the Canadian tour leader, who could open the odd-looking locks on several of the ships' Soviet-era doors. Just the right pressure and a certain indescribable flick of the wrist were all it took me to unravel the secret of the round locks with their half-moon keys that defeated everyone else. With those anachronistic marvels of Russian engineering I was right at home, as I had mastered the same locks on my office door several continents away, in distant Kazakhstan.

How did you do it? the steward asked, as I popped open the door he could not seduce.

Now I Can Sit With the Old Men

Easy. It is an acquired expertise. I do it at work every day.........

And there was the Russian stealth massage, behind quiet whispers and the shrouded exchange of the most universal language of all: cold, hard cash. My muscles were tired and my shoulders were sore as I held the accumulated stress of too many months of way-too-long hours at work. But I found a therapeutic, if clandestine, massage when my handful of Russian vocabulary brought a smile to the faces of the women who straightened our cabins each day. Normally out of sight, just a shadow that like a phantom slips in to clean when we step out, *Lidia's* face lit up when I could at least say *hello* and *thank you* in a language whose words she knew as her own. A short conversation about living in a neighboring Central Asian country she had once considered a friend, and a bit of extra cash brought me the strong hands and firm fingers that my tightened shoulders craved, though she would have been fired if her boss had found out.

No visit to Antarctica would have been complete without seeing the penguins, without observing those most endearing of creatures, the most optimistic in the animal kingdom, the most playful in this land of bitter cold. Once again I could learn a lesson about faith, humor, and courage in the face of adversity in my travels. Nature, not man, was my teacher this time, embodied by a group of adorably photogenic birds. Their playful spirit brings humor to a place where life is deadly serious and the penalty for a failure, a miscalculation, or a mishap can easily and quickly be someone's swift and painful demise. Within moments of sitting quietly near a penguin-covered hill, the flightless creatures were no longer merely the distant object of our rapt attention, elegant in their simple attire of black and white. We were now the focus of theirs. Within moments of sitting down in silent contemplation on the hard-frozen ground, my bright red jacket a visual siren for all to see, a bevy of *Adelies* waddled over to within a foot of where I quietly sat. They approached. They stood. They scrutinized. They observed. In a game of turnabout-is-fair-play, it was me in the animal pen at the zoo this time, and they were the gawking crowd.

200

Was I really in Antarctica? Was I really there? I asked myself as an army of penguins circled me, parading about with their affable personalities, their inquisitive nature and their dramatic black and white coats.

Antarctica. Was this real? I asked myself as a sea of penetrating dark eyes surveyed every aspect of my presence, watched my every move.

What was this place, really? I considered as I reflected on the scenery around me and I recorded the penguins' curious looks. No doubt they asked themselves the same, looking at me.

Was this a figment of my imagination? Or was I a figment of theirs?

This excursion was the trip of a lifetime. Antarctica was a captivating, inspiring, humbling place. But, not unlike in Namibia with its vastness and its beauty, it was with a complicated mix of elation, guilt, and awe that I looked back at those handsome birds that were looking so curiously at me. Even with the greatest of efforts to minimize our impact, we human intruders leave an undeniable footprint on this breathtaking land where the gods of winter work and play, where the forces of nature reign supreme, where Nature ultimately has the last laugh. With some twelve to fifteen thousand visitors to the Southern Ocean and the Antarctic region each year, we humans cannot help but leave some unintended, unwanted, damaging traces behind. How high is the yet uncalculated price of our visits? Only time will tell.

Was I really in Antarctica, this magnificent, art-filled land, where spirits ride the waves and play on the spray of the whales? Replete with telling names like Elephant Island, Deception Island, Hell's Gate, and Paradise Bay, I asked myself. Had I really journeyed where the gods court the adventurous, and the wind- and weather-fed titans clash? Where nations come together to protect the sanctity of nature while they draw swords and drop bombs over lesser issues in other places on earth. Where the wind, the water, and the sun can bless but they can also curse. Was this reality, or was I just sleepwalking through my dream?

In the end, *who could say, really, what this was?* Barry Lopez asked of Antarctica's cousin to the far north. *What was this place, really?* At times it felt like a photograph, like my imagination, like a dream, but indeed, Antarctica was a prism through which I saw not just the infinite color spectrum of blue and white. It was not just the lens through which I saw the beauty of virgin ice and snow. Rather, Antarctica was the window through which I finally understood the enormity of nature on a whole new scale. It was the aperture through which I gained a new perspective on the meaning of global warming and *greenhouse gas*, on the importance of preserving the environment and the impact of failing to do so. *What was this place really?* Antarctica was an unexpectedly instructive prism of ice and snow.

America after *Nine One One*

The United States (2001)

For some minutes Alice stood without speaking,
looking out in all directions over the country –
and a most curious country it was.

Lewis Carroll, *Through the Looking Glass*
and What Alice Found There

ootless was the word some used to describe me after ten years of a vagabond life. Skipping from one corner of the world to another. Working here, working there. Sashaying from one country to the next on the wings of a plane and the pages of a fat and tattered passport. Like the malaria parasite, this gypsy lifestyle was now in my blood.

But ten years of living out of a suitcase without a consistent roof over my head was, even for me, a long time. *It was time to settle down* I told friends. So I bought a house in the American Southwest. In the country, if not the land, of my birth. In the searing heat and beige-colored sand and gravel and rock of yet another desert that calls my name. There, the giant *Saguaro* cacti march across the landscape. They are the foot soldiers of a distant time, the Native Americans in the area believe. There, the midnight skies glitter with the lights of a million stars. And a thousand lightning strikes dance and arc across the dark slate blue of a late afternoon monsoon, making my telephone flash and ring. There, ancient spirits ride the winds, rise with the sun, and fall with the snow; a giant, poisonous toad twice the size of my closed fist took up residence outside my front door. A lizard moved into my bathroom, and two scorpions raced across my living room floor, coming to an abrupt halt just in front of my feet. This bit of paradise is unquestionably the most beautiful corner of the United States.

A few days after moving there, I stopped by the local fire station. It sat just three-quarters of a mile from my house. Inside, I came face to face with two big men and an eye-catching poster that I could not ignore. Not a picture of a stunning southern Arizona sunset, the distinctive silhouette of the *Saguaro* that make this place unique, or a wildflower in bloom, but a collage of every sort of rattlesnake that calls the *Sonora* Desert its home. The same place *I* came to call home. These were my neighbors: short, slender, long, skinny, fat. There were about eight or ten varieties, as I recall.

Can we help you?

I smiled and pointed to the glossy-paper, full-color photos of the gravel-colored snakes.

"Do you know about our Desert Pest Removal Program?" one deep voice watching me asked.

I had just learned about it the day before.

But surely in a neighborhood like this you don't get many calls, I thought silently to myself.

I was in for a big surprise.

In the previous twelve months these firemen had collected over *six thousand* rattlesnakes from peoples' garages, yards, even one or two in the living room inside someone's house.

"*Usually* those are people who leave their doors open," he said in a relaxed, matter-of-fact way.

Leave your door open in country where poisonous snakes abound? I wondered in awe at the things people do.

"Where do you live?" the other voice beside me asked.

I told him my address. It turns out he knew it well. When it comes to one who captures venomous snakes for living that is not necessarily a good sign.

"I live two streets over from you. Last year I had five rattlesnakes in my garage," he said with a smile on his face and a bounce in his voice.

Those were bragging rights I felt no need to earn.

"If you see any snakes at your place, just give us a call. We've collected them every month of the year. Just had a call last week, in fact, and here we are only ten days 'til Christmas."

That made my day.

Wasn't I afraid to move to Arizona with the rattlesnakes? my neighbors asked.

I could have turned the same question back on them, as their houses were right next to mine.

I had lived with poisonous snakes as neighbors for much of the previous ten years. Cobras and Vipers in Mali where a small terra cotta-colored snake with its unmistakable triangular head lay coiled in my path as I walked along a gravel road early one cool March day. *Mambas* and Bushmasters in Botswana, where the dried translucent skin shed by an unknown variety of legless reptile graced a bush in my very small yard. A Canadian acquaintance in Ghana where I had lived for a year and a half had changed houses after finding the eighth *Mamba* in her yard. In West Africa they call it the *Two-Step Snake*. They say if a *Mamba* strikes, you can take just two steps before you fall dead.

There were *Kraits* and venomous vine snakes in Cambodia and Viet Nam where I walked barefoot in the rice paddies and waded waist-high in the flood waters. Cobras sleep, as I did, on the sand of the *Thar* Desert in *Rajasthan*. And the deadly *Fer de Lance* made its home nearby as I slept on the damp Costa Rican ground. I had seen plenty of live poisonous snakes in the wild myself, and I had seen the skins of many more. I knew first-hand of individuals who died from toxic bites. I had listened to countless reports of gardeners I knew exercising a swift hand and a sharp knife. Poisonous snakes, for me, were nothing new.

But six thousand in twelve months? That's five hundred a month. *On average, sixteen every day.* Just do the math. *What had I done?*

"Don't open your garage door," Handyman Bob said when he arrived at my house.

I looked at him squarely and enquired *why not.*

"You've got a rattlesnake there."

No longer interested in the shelves or mirror I had called him to hang, I grabbed my cell phone and went outside for a look. It was a sunny morning with a vivid, clear, blue sky. Bob followed in close pursuit.

A beauty with a striking pattern in chocolate, khaki, and tan lay at the base of my garage door, peaceful in the shadow of my house. His triangular head lay somewhere inside the garage. I could see nearly three feet of thick, richly marked tail. I could see an inch and a half of bone-colored rattles fashionably accessorizing the tip. Quick shivers marched rhythmically up my spine as I stood in the warm mid-morning southern Arizona sun.

Desert Pest Removal, I remembered, and turned my fingers loose to dance across the face plate of my phone. I felt the muscles in my chest constrict. I felt my stomach tighten and my skin grow cold.

In roughly six minutes the firemen arrived. Two good-looking, muscular, brown-haired men in heavy, black boots, bright yellow pants, and navy t-shirts strode confidently up my drive. They had parked their chartreuse truck right in front of my house, ensuring I would soon be the talk of the other people living on my street.

Inside my garage they snared the neck just behind the head. Ready to run I'm not sure where, I pushed the button that raised the garage door, glad I could stand fifteen feet back. *Fight or flight* at the onset of danger. I know in that instance what I would do.

The firemen held my rattlesnake up. A novice at these things, I had expected to see it struggle to get free, to writhe and twist in anger and frustration and fear. But there he hung. Straight as a plumb line. Silent as a mouse. Limp as a wet rag. Dead.

Dead.

Dead.

I had not only performed an astonishing feat of precision I would be incapable of any other day, but I had broken Arizona state law. Without even knowing he was there, I had lowered the garage door on this snake just right behind his head in an unparalleled act of impeccable timing. Without even knowing he was there, I had squeezed the life out of this *legally protected* 'desert pest.' Having run an early morning errand, I had put my car in the garage just an hour before. Evidently my unfortunate visitor lay in wait on the gravel close by, like an actor waiting in the wings, ready to make his theatrical debut.

Sensing warmth from the interior of my garage, this cold-blooded creature mechanically sought refuge from the chilled pre-dawn, mid-September desert air. He muscled forward toward the warmth the genes of his ancestors told him would soothe his frigid bones. Instead, playing out on the modern stage of man overtaking nature's shrinking desert space, he found an early and most unfortunate curtain call, a *guillotine* of sorts. My legs trembled briefly as I reflected on what I, and my garage door, had just done.

Someone told me later I could have sold the snake for two hundred dollars. *Two hundred dollars*, I regretted, for an instant until my senses returned. *Stand on the corner of South Tucson hawking a dead rattlesnake, hoping to find just the right person who wanted a new leather belt that day, or a band for his hat?* I don't think so.

Over the course of the next several months and following few years I saw countless other snakes. Thankfully not the six thousand of the firemen's log, but a hungry Black Racer in the bird cage at the *Desert Museum*. He was watching, with a calculating eye, a miniature owl sitting petrified on the highest branch in its cage, its piercing eyes trained on the menace below. A stunning black and white California King Snake whipped across the road in front of my car during a nearly blinding monsoon. Its distinctive black and white bands showed clearly despite the pelting rain. I saw numerous road kills, and two snakes mating in the middle of a street near my house. They resembled a large, loose, contorted ball of yarn. A baby snake wiggled across the bricks just in front of my toes as I knocked on a friend's front door. No bigger than a pencil, he was an out-of-season surprise in the chilled, early October night. And one Rattler lay straight as a rod on the warm pavement of another mid-fall day, flicking his tongue furiously in and out as I stopped my little, low-riding, top-down convertible car to take a closer look. I remembered the driver I used in Namibia who said the snakes on the road rise up and wrap themselves around the undercarriage of the passing cars, eventually working their way inside. I never learned if it is true.

But the big prize came twenty minutes before I was expecting a house full of guests.

I stood briefly on my back patio. Darryl, the yard man who kept my roses watered and my weeds in check, was standing next to me and we were discussing the monotony of a schedule for the drip system he had recently installed. All was quiet in the late afternoon sun as a hawk passed overhead, silently riding the transparent blue currents of the soft desert air. Then the very slightest of movement caught my attention less than five feet in front of my eyes.

"There's a rattlesnake," I said, surprised at the site coming into laser-sharp focus and the words coming out of my mouth.

I pointed as the beige and tan of the gravel that made up my desert landscape yard began to move again slowly, just a few feet from where we stood.

His head rose less than an inch, his tail slid forward ever so very slightly. There in my yard, just an uncomfortably few short feet from Darryl and me, was a *Western Diamondback*, the largest of the rattlesnakes in the Western United States. He had handsome rattles and bold markings that blended perfectly with the desert floor that happened to be my back yard. For all my years of watching for snakes of varying colors and patterns in many parts of the world, I was caught off guard by this master of camouflage. Had he not moved, I would have never seen this poisonous snake that lay so remarkably close to my feet.

Rattlesnakes aside, the desert is a surprising wonderland rich in *flora* and *fauna* few who have not seen it appreciate. Birds of prey soared overhead as masters of the sky and much of the universe below. *Don't leave babies, cats, or small dogs alone outside,* I had been told when I first arrived. *They may be snatched from above.*

Coyotes sang at night in a chorus that carried so far I first thought the teenagers in the neighborhood were having an all-night party and a very noisy time, at four-thirty a.m. A Roadrunner skipped up my front yard and looked at me with a cocked head. Families of quail routinely trotted across the roads. I spotted a tarantula crossing the road twenty feet ahead of my car. And a bear stopped mid-morning traffic one day, in an intersection not far from my house.

And each March the land transformed into an artist's palette as the gods of Spring called forth an army of flowers, painting the beige, gray, and tan of the arid land with brilliant splashes of pink, purple, apricot, orange, gold, and red. In seasonal splendor, they rivaled the brightest Thai silk, the most creatively colored Indian *saris,* or any child's sixty-four color *Crayola* box as brilliant wildflowers burst forth from the ground.

It was not long after I illegally killed the rattlesnake at my garage that the police showed up unexpectedly at my house.

There was a knock on my door around eleven p.m., in a neighborhood where people retire early and individuals don't just drop by.

Who's there, please? I asked through the closed and locked front door.

It's the police.

The police? My heart skipped a beat and my brain moved fast. *What were these officers doing at my house?*

This was in the early days after *September 11, 2001,* when U.S. flags multiplied like rabbits, and most Americans lived in a new-found fear of the foreign *jihadi,* the domestic terrorist, and the man or woman next door. And there I stood with my passport full of strange destinations and Arabic stamps. There I sat with tales from afar, from questionable corners of a now-believed-to-be-sinister world. With a lifestyle and career that few shared and very few others could understand. *What kind of work do you do?* people always asked me, looking slightly askance.

And the police now stood unexpectedly at my door.

There I was in the shadow of *September Eleventh*, with friends who managed bank mergers and the electronic webs they create. With a suitor who oversaw the building of America's big airplanes, and a close friend who drove Europe's high-speed trains. There I was, having lived in the path of shady narco-traffickers and money launderers abroad. And there I was, having vacationed many times alone in the Middle East. There I stood, having been paid for my international contracts by wire transfers more than once. Having bought my house for cash. Having inexplicably moved close to where one of the World Trade Center hijackers reportedly learned to fly, and where an *Al Qaeda* sleeper cell allegedly sat. And I had just recently rewritten my will.

Only days before I had been questioned by the *FBI*. They had not only telephoned me numerous times but they came to my home to ask about a private e-mail I had recently received. *How did they even know?* Their visit gave me nightmares, but not until four years later did the media make public the extent to which the U.S. Government had, in the new millennium, been watching its citizens, listening to their phone conversations, and reading their electronic mail.

The police. *September eleventh.* The FBI. In this new era of fear and terror and intrigue, life in the United States had become a bit surreal. I was used to being watched overseas. I was accustomed to being monitored. To being *handled*, and *minded*, and observed. But in my own country it was something new. I had grown up in a land where the press was free. Where the government was transparent. Where individuals did not quiet their own voice out of fear for who was watching, listening, reading. I found these new changes unsettling. They were the subject of spy novels and conspiracy theories and fiction movies, and secretive conversations with trusted colleagues overseas. They were not historically the substance or the flavor of my own homeland. Now, in my own country they were giving me pause. In the nascent domestic climate of vigilantism and fear, I began to look at my own country with new eyes. And it looked uncomfortably strange.

"May I come in?" the policeman asked.

"Is there a reason why you're here?" I asked in return, as my mind raced through the new atmosphere that had swept across America from the White House to the West, threatening to turn reason, common sense, and the founding principles of my homeland dangerously upside down.

"Did you call the police?" the navy blue shirt, black hair, shiny badge, and brightly polished shoes asked as I peered through the security door.

I had not called the police.

"No. But I was trying to call China," I said, a bit bewildered by the events transpiring at my front door.

It had been only two weeks before that the *FBI* finally made contact with me in the far southwestern reaches of that vast Asian land where I had gone to visit friends.

"Isn't it a little late to call China?" the policeman asked, with more than a hint of sarcasm in his voice.

No, not at all, I replied like a robot with a mechanical rhythm to my words, not skipping even a beat.

The time difference makes it early in the morning there while it is late at night here, blah, blah, blah, blah, blah.

I rattled on as if it were the most normal thing in the world. In fact, to me with my international life and my globetrotting ways, it was.

A blank look faced me through my decorative metal screen door. It was then I realized the problem and I tried hard not to laugh, in this new era of suspicion, of the United States President advising the *UPS* delivery man to report unusual activity, and saying Mr and Mrs Smith should tell the authorities of the activities of their neighbors next door.

I was raised to trust my government, to be proud of my country. I believe in the values America's Founding Fathers put forth. But increasingly I began to wonder, as I rested in the shadow of the giant *Saguaro* cacti that stand sentry over a sacred past, what those early men would think if they dropped in for a visit today.

It was only after Monica Lewinsky's blue dress inundated my television screen in Kazakhstan for weeks and months on end, half a world away from the White House and the happenings within, that I had realized how fortunate I have been to be raised in a country where speech has been unfettered and where the government was usually honest. I thanked the lottery of the gene pool that I had been born in America, the land of liberty where the *First Amendment* was written to protect free speech, the courts were generally fair, and the governmental checks and balances of our earliest days usually worked.

For years I had been living and working in countries where colleagues of mine whispered to me of their neighbors disappearing in the night for things they had written or said. I had lived and worked where the press was muzzled and journalists were routinely murdered, imprisoned, threatened, or harassed. Where some people will not converse with others, simply out of fear. I had lived and worked in countries where due process is fiction and the right to legal representation is just a dream. But it chilled my bones when well-educated American friends of mine said they no longer speak their political minds, not in some far-off country or foreign land, but in their own country. In mine. In the Land of the Free and the Home of the Brave. In the United States. *What was happening*, I wondered, *to the proud, free nation I once knew?*

The police. The new political order. The world after *Nine One One*. The change in mentality and attitude, and the new red-, white-, and blue-striped ways. To many they offered comfort, to others they raised concern. To me in my own country they seemed disconcertingly, uncomfortably, alarmingly odd.

It was there in this changing post-*911* landscape that the police knocked on my door at eleven o'clock that night. I had, in what turned out to be a comedy of errors, called the police myself, though I did not immediately realize it at the time. In my efforts to call China from the phone in my house I stumbled over the unfamiliar codes of the American telephone system I rarely used. In my attempts, in vain, to call outside the United States, I tripped numerous times over the puzzle of the codes to dial internationally. So accustomed to dialing *nine* for an outside line at the myriad hotels around the world that are my homes away from home, I had, in fact, dialed the emergency response number, *911*. The policemen at my front step were simply responding to my call. But in the new era of fear, the new kaleidoscope of conspiracy theories and panic and domestic security concerns, I, too, had fallen prey to seeing the bogey man where he did not exist.

Days later I was busy looking at fabrics at a local sewing store when I sensed someone's eyes on mine. I looked up but I did not recognize the face. Dark hair in a ragged, 1960s-era beatnik cut. Dark eyes framed with wire rims. A hint of Asia in his eyes. A touch of Moscow in his dark clothes. He was clearly watching me but nothing came up in the normally reliable *Rolodex* that fills my brain as I flipped quickly through the thousands of invisible business cards I hold. He said nothing as he continued to look at me intently. But my search for something recognizable once again came up blank. I looked back down at the fabrics in my hands. He turned and walked away. And five minutes later he returned, but this time he called my name.

Margaret? he said.

I stopped in my tracks and looked up once again. This man was clearly out of place. He did not fit the profile of the store's usual clientele. His accent was strange. His words were broken and few. Yet there he stood, calling me by my name.

"I'm *Agaze*," he said. "Do you remember me?"

What a small, if strange, world it is. *Agaze*. The brother of a woman I knew years earlier in Kazakhstan. I had worked with her; I had drunk vodka and tea and eaten rice with their parents in their tired Soviet apartment in their tiny forgotten village in the *Tien Shen* Mountains on the far edge of a now very-distant southern Kazakhstan town. It all came tumbling back. *Agaze*. I had worked very, very briefly with him. Years before and thousands of miles away. With my few words of Russian and his few words of English we managed to schedule a dinner at my house for the following night.

What are you doing?

You're having guests for dinner?

You fly to Cambodia the very next day, at five a.m.

How can you do it? friends asked.

How can I not? I replied.

Agaze came over to dine just hours before I flew halfway around the world yet again.

His parents did not say, *sorry, not now, we're busy*, when I would show up unannounced at their door. Instead they always invited me in without even a fraction of a second of hesitation, generously offering me tea and food, whatever their pantry happened to hold. Now it was my turn to do the same. I was raised in a family that welcomed foreigners into our home. The relatively recent American idea of saying I was too busy to be hospitable was a totally alien concept, and to me, very strange. And so *Agaze* and friends dined with me in my house even if my friends and neighbors found it untimely or odd.

Manual Komroff's *Introduction* to *The Travels of Marco Polo* describes the famed Venetian merchant's return home, when after twenty-six years he barely found his old street in Venice, and his old house. There, *after the Deserts of Persia, the lofty steeps of Pamir, and mysterious Tibet*, Marco Polo's clothes looked strange to his neighbors and his accent had changed. The dogs reportedly barked as he knocked on the door of his own house, after an absence of many years. Save a few distinguishing details, that story could have been mine.

Like Marco Polo, and Lewis Carroll's *Alice in Wonderland*, I came to look around myself in Arizona, having now lived more than ten years abroad. What I saw of my own country was different than what I used to know; it was at once both familiar and strange. It was the nation of my birth. It was the land of my citizenship. It was the place I ultimately call home. It was at once a place I understood and a place I no longer knew. The United States after many of my travels overseas. And America after *Nine One One*.

What a most curious country my own homeland now had become. The United States. My country. My home. It had changed with its recent terrorist events. *And so, in my travels,* I learned, *had I.*

Things That Go *Boom!* In The Night

Iraq (2007)

Go placidly amid the noise and the haste
and remember what peace there may be in silence.

Max Ehrmann, *Desiderata*

*T*hirteen. Fourteen. Fifteen. Sixteen…..The number continued to climb as a deepening crescendo echoed through the black of the night. Ice-cold tremors roared down my spine and my jaw locked tight. Each new volley shook the floor with deadly force. Spears of shrapnel pierced the air with lightening speed and lethal intent. It was just past eleven o'clock in early July. The night had just begun. And we were being mortared once again.

In my five months in Iraq I did not collect the war stories of some; I did not *see it all*. I did not experience the full brutality of the war. Not even close. I was not a soldier on the front lines of combat. I was not a doctor in the hospital that received the wounded, nor a journalist reporting on the blood and the gore. I am not an Iraqi fearing for my life. Though I heard them, I did not witness the car bombs and improvised explosive devices and, the explosively-formed penetrators, nor the vehicle-born *IEDs*. If I am lucky, I never will.

But I did live with the bunkers, the alarms, the explosions, the sand bags and rockets and mortars and guns. I saw the palaces-turned rubble, held the shrapnel, saw the bullet holes, the scars. Colleagues in my office

221

received terrifyingly credible death threats and others had extraordinarily close calls. People I met have since been killed. In five very short, very long months I heard the sounds of the insurgency, the deafening, cavernous explosions that rocked my world, the fire fights, the deadly jack-hammer rat-a-tat-tat-tat-tat-tat. I saw the skeletal vestiges of *Shock and Awe*. Like millions, I watched the regularly regurgitated reports on *CNN* and *BBC*. I also heard many that did not make the televised news. And I lived daily with the anxiety, the apprehension, the anticipation, and the dread.

Early on, I learned not to look too far into a future that might not come. I learned to take just one day at a time. After five months, I came home scratched, abraded, scuffed, tired, and worn. But I came home stronger. Today I am more gracious. I am more humble, more politicized, more thankful, and more sad.

Even after just five months it was hard to shake the haunting sounds of mortars and car bombs that reverberated in my brain. Even as I rested for a few days in the luxurious folds of a serenely quiet Jordanian hotel, with gentle music, a salt bath, sheets smooth as butter, and a feather and down-soft bed that promised to transport me safely through the night, I caught myself listening with one ear for that next loud boom that would in a fraction of one split second shatter any temporary, hard-won sense of safety and calm. The bogey man was no longer a shadowy figure snatching children in the night; He was the mortar, the rocket, the car bomb, the explosively-formed-penetrator, the rocket-propelled grenade. Even in Jordan I jumped if a door shut hard. Even in the safe distance of Amman I caught myself, as I retired at night, feeling anxious that I could not dive underneath the low frame of the night's exquisitely comfortable bed.

If it is in the face of adversity that we grow, then I grew a bit in Iraq. For the first time in my life I began to count my blessings not just occasionally, but each and every day. And I considered every new sunrise a gift. Working mostly behind cement T-walls, fortified checkpoints, armored vehicles, and heavily armed guards, what I experienced was the low-calorie, low-sodium, *lite* version of this war. I can only imagine the nightmares of those in uniform. As a civilian I went outside *the wire,* outside the heavily fortified compound gate, only from time to time; they did it every day.

I think of the Iraqis I met and I can only begin to imagine their living hell. I can only fathom a fraction of the experience of the men and women and children of Iraq who did not ask for this insurgency, this terror, this carnage, this war. In Oslo I met a young Norwegian woman who interviewed asylum-seeking refugees from Iraq. She said she never thought she would see an Arab man cry, but she saw it every day. *Each one thinks he is the only one;* but she said the refugees, *they all cry* at what they fear, what they have seen, what they have lived, and what they have lost.

"They *all* cry," she said, "the men, the women; they all cry."

"And they each think they are alone in their tears."

I did not go to Iraq to fight, to win, or to lose. I did not go for politics or praise. I did not go to Iraq for America's *Homeland Security.* I did not go because someone required me to; I went of my own free will. I did not go to Iraq out of any sense of patriotism or economic need or monetary greed. I went for one very determined, very frustrated, very private conviction. I went not for, but *because of* the war.

In Iraq, as I read or heard each new report of a car bomb that senselessly murdered and destroyed, a new barrage of mortars, an increase in insurgent attacks, I wondered why I risked my life and the lives of others whose only job it was to protect the likes of me. I watched, as I rode through town, how the other vehicles veered to the shoulder, racing off the road in fear of my oncoming personal security detail, my *PSD,* that heavily-armed bubble designed to get me home alive. I wondered in those moments whether I was doing the right thing. When I faced the many and vast challenges of my economic development work, I wondered if that tremendously uphill battle was the best use of my talents, my experience, my time. But when I looked down from the helicopters and saw the hopeful, smiling faces of the

Iraqi children looking up as they waved, I knew why I was there, and I knew it was the right, albeit very dangerous, place for me to be.

For decades I have not chosen the safe roads; I have not shrunk away from risk. I have known for years in many of the places I have chosen to travel, to live, or to work, that there are countless scores of people who wish nothing greater than for me, as an American, to be dead. It is a sadly political fact. It was not, however, until that early July night at about 11:10 p.m., that I faced head-on for the first time a darker, more starkly, resolutely sinister truth.

It was not collateral damage I heard as I counted the incoming mortars that rained down one after another outside my trailer door, each with a horrific thunderous boom that rocked the previously still mid-summer Iraqi night. That concussive pounding was not the sound of someone just *passively* wanting me to die as it shook my trailer floor. It was not the sound of indirect fire targeted at someone else as was daily the case when I worked in Baghdad's infamous *International Zone*, the infamous *IZ;* our compound out in the provinces was too small for such a salvo to be chance. It was not something lethal intended for someone else. It was the brutally explosive sledge hammer of individuals aligning my trailer in their cross-hairs as I lay silently under my bed. They were trying with hatefully deliberate aim to annihilate my colleagues and me, to turn us into blood-soaked dust. It was a sobering, indisputable fact that dug craters, broke windows, ruptured sewer lines, sprayed shrapnel, and pock-marked the trailers less than fifty feet from mine just after eleven o'clock that otherwise ordinary night. That fifteen-minute stretch of the sand-clouded Iraqi evening was a clarifying, seismic, defining moment as I lay wondering if that quarter-hour represented the remainder of my life. People did not just passively want me dead; *they were trying to do the job.*

It was a sinking, lonely feeling by myself in my trailer as I tried hard to meld with the linoleum under my bed. Shuddering as I counted each successive mortar that hit, I wondered how long the deafening assault would last. But even as I felt very isolated in the midst of that attack, in fact I was not alone. I saw clearly on the silent faces at breakfast the next morning that others were profoundly shaken just like me. I heard it in the water-cooler conversations. I knew it when the security guards asked me with an unparalleled gentleness and concern if I were *OK*, if I had been alone, if I had been afraid. I heard it echo in their uncharacteristically quiet conversations over cereal and eggs.

It had been a few weeks since we had last been attacked.

The hours and days without the mortars and rockets and car bombs were a blessing of incomprehensibly immense proportions. But rest, however alluringly, tantalizingly seductive, remained for me maddeningly out of reach. It was ironic that those seemingly normal moments in reality brought a heightened sense of vulnerability, insecurity, and foreboding that increased with each new, uneventful day. It was both funny and sad how in that environment of uncertainty I came to distrust the quiet that should have been my solace, my minister, my friend. Instead of finding comfort in the pockets of tranquility, I bumped against its limits, I ran headlong into its ceilings and its walls. We knew it was only a matter of time before the unspoken truce that gave us momentary silence would be broken once again. My colleagues and I could not enjoy the quiet for we wondered with darkness when it would end. We knew with regrettable certainty that the silence could not last. Instead of enjoying the respite, we pondered the calendar looking for the next assault, thinking we had been spared too many days. Platitudes aside, it is hard to stop and smell the roses when you are waiting, on edge, for the other shoe to drop.

"*Don't get complacent,*" I heard in the shadow of a whisper as I talked with others in the hall.

"*We're overdue,*" my colleagues murmured.

"*It has been quiet too long,*" was another cynical way of expressing the same thing; it was a comment that was voiced repeatedly with chilling truth.

As if trying to cheat a jinx, we did not speak those words freely. We did not speak them in a strong voice; we did not really want them to be heard as if we feared they might somehow trigger the response we all cursed. Instead those words were intimations offered in hushed tones to trusted members of our secret club, in furtive conversations, under carefully-guarded breath. We spoke them only in whispers as if the mere act of giving voice to our worries might invoke the vigorous wrath of those who wished to kill us, of those who would have too gladly celebrated our premature death. It was as if we were skirting the edges of black magic. As if the mere mention of an attack might bring one on.

We played games nearly every day; we counted the numbers, we counted the hours and the days since the last attack. *Would today be the day? Would tonight be the night?* We disguised our apprehension. We masked our experiences, perhaps as much for ourselves as for those we love. Even while we kept our e-mails short and our phone conversations light, we wondered if tonight we would have *the big one*, if only because it had been quiet too long. Because the scorching temperatures of the sweltering Middle Eastern summer rose another few degrees, to one hundred thirty-six, or because that day the sky was unusually clear. Because it was a particularly significant religious day. Because someone was arrested, or someone else was not. Because of any reason, or no reason at all.

There was no magic predictive formula that worked for us every time. There was no higher math that told us with some certainty when the next indirect fire would come, or the next direct attack. There was no equation that told us in advance when to run at break-neck speed for the bunkers, or that allowed us to correctly set our watches to throw on our flak jackets and dive under our beds. And so we continued our vigilance and our fantasies and our illusions and our games. I counted myself infinitely lucky that my site was spared from mortars and rockets far more than it was not, and far more than most. But I also lived with the knowledge that like the flip of a switch, that could change at any time.

In the reality that framed my life in Iraq, I grew accustomed to the sight of firearms everywhere I went. I stood side by side with men and women holding very big guns. The side arms that elsewhere make my blood go cold, in Iraq helped allay my fear. When I was *outside the wire*, I rode and walked in a bullet-proof vest and helmet, surrounded by a very heavily armed *PSD*. The firepower I saw before some meetings I attended would make international drug cartels tip their heads in respect. I took comfort in the presence of those firearms even as I recoiled at their sight.

I ran on a treadmill almost daily to reduce the tension. I lifted weights to build my strength. Still, a slippery, stealthy, invisible thief stole a little of my heart and my soul each day. Ever present, inescapable, invisible, stress took its toll, leaving me increasingly fatigued at the end of each week. I did not have gentle dreams when I slept any more. In fact, I did not dream at all. I could count the days since I had slept soundly through the night. The numbers were not so hard to do. I just had to turn the calendar back in time to the day I arrived in Iraq.

People asked me if I was scared and I even asked myself. I did not feel consciously afraid even as I pondered the dangers, as I considered the risks. But I knew all the same, that at some inner, primordial, subterranean, subcutaneous, subconscious level I was. I did not feel it in my waking hours, but I saw it in my sleep. For one who has been blessed with the ability to slumber soundly anywhere, on anything, at any time, I never dozed off more than two or three hours straight. Some nights it was just one hour before I awakened wide-eyed, tired but unable to fall back to sleep. Those nights the hours dragged on. I took sad comfort in knowing that I was not alone even though no one shared my trailer or my bed. For when I asked most others, their story was the same.

People who knew me told me I was strong. But like the river that gradually erodes a piece of granite over time, the encroaching tension and ensuing fatigue wore me down a little bit each day. As the days became weeks and the weeks turned to months, I looked around myself to see how others coped, to learn what strategies they employed to beat the enemy within, the parasite that ate slowly away at us all. We came from different countries, different professions, different experiences, different cities, and different states. But we faced a common, undisputed foe. And in that crystallizing experience that is today's deadly Iraq, we shared a fraternal bond, however grand or dubious in honor, which will go with us to our graves.

I looked to my foreign colleagues who had been through this all before in their own homelands, but they did not have the answers on how to beat the stress that ground away at us each and every day. They, too, were just trying to keep going to and through the next day. I looked to the military men and women with their training and their guns, but they did not have the answer any more than I did. I looked to those who were older, with the wisdom of their years, and I looked to those with the resilience and optimism of youth. But the magic elixir of peace within did not discriminate; it eluded us all.

In this life that no one should lead, the threat of rockets and mortars colored my every move. I slept in pajamas, and my showers were purposely quick. I kept my phone calls home unpredictable and short, not wanting to raise alarm if on a particular day I could not call, not wanting to have to explain the violent sounds my family might unexpectedly hear at the other end of the line.

I read a little each evening, but my attention span was appallingly short. I tried to watch an engaging movie on television but my mind wandered. I tried to write a journal but the words would not come. I knew this was the cost of staying unconsciously, surreptitiously in a state of always-ready alert, but I passed it off, I *sucked it up*, I raised my head and went forward through another day as did everyone else. I often awoke with my jaw clenched tight but I shook it loose and went running on the treadmill yet again, trying with only limited success to mitigate what grew inside me a little more each and every day.

The religious among us took comfort and strength in their faith, but I do not know whether prayers work. I do not know whether anyone listens or anyone responds. I do not know whether there is some great being in the heavens or the sky. In fact when I have looked at the scars in so many countries where I have worked, I wonder how, if there is a *God*, he can so often be asleep at the wheel. I do not know whether there is some higher power, and if so, of which faith he is. But in Iraq I did not once take off the knotted red cord that hung around my neck. Even in the shower I wore that talisman from the Buddhist monk who blessed me in Bhutan earlier in the year. I fingered it several times a day, and every night before I slept, taking comfort in its presence and holding on to the hope that its power would keep me safe, or would at least transport me with speed and give me peace. Though I am not Catholic, I cherish the sets of Rosary beads some of my foreign friends gave me in Iraq, one a very dear gift from a mother to her son, who in turn gave it to me. And I learned that the simple act of watching my Bhutanese prayer flags flutter on the wings of my air conditioner's breeze helped me breathe a little easier and a little stronger each day.

I knew where my flak jacket, helmet, radio, and boots were at all times. And I kept them within arm's reach at night. I asked myself each evening whether I wanted to sleep on my bed, or on the hard floor underneath, as many others did. Each night I played the odds like *Russian Roulette*, of whether the next mortar would shoot through my ceiling or my wall at lightning speed, piercing my bed and me with deadly shrapnel before I would have time to dive for cover. *Do I tempt fate and sleep on my bed with one ear listening for that first sickeningly loud explosion that catalyzes me to catapult myself to the floor, diving for cover before the next mortar hits, all the while telling myself I must not live in fear? Or do I better my odds and lie flat and low underneath my bed, hoping in some presumption of protective cover, for a good night's sleep?* Nightly, it was a personal debate.

Is it easier to give way to worry from the start, or to awaken with a jolt to a siren that shatters the air and shoots red-hot adrenalin coursing through my veins? Will I sleep better on the softness of a mattress a few feet up, one ear trained to the darkness of the night? Or will I sleep longer on an unforgiving hardness that reconfigures the trigonometry of shrapnel spray, knowing my mattress does not give comfort beneath my weary back but believing it may offer some limited measure of protection overhead, no matter how tenuous or false? With a good night's sleep just out of reach, those nightly questions were a roll of the dice I never conquered.

I wrote home to my family and friends, but I did not tell them much. Perhaps my silence spoke louder than my words, but I did not tell them I had my blood type written on my helmet, my flak jacket, and the heels of both boots, or that it was the first question I had to answer to ride in a *PSD* or to take the helicopters to my site and back. I did not tell them I had to officially list any identifying scars and tattoos that might enable the identification of severed body parts. Or that a particularly notorious sniper had just moved into our part of town. I did not tell them the number of *duck and covers* we had. I did not tell them that each time I left our compound, even in a heavily-armed *PSD*, I knew that at someone else's whim I might easily not make it back alive. I did not tell them the grim reality of working as a civilian in the midst of this very costly war.

Although they asked me what it was like, I did not write my family and friends about the mortars and rockets and wondering if the vehicle I was about to pass up ahead masked a car bomb or an *IED*. I wrote the *Baghdad Fashion Forecast* instead, saying khaki was the season's newest hot-weather look; I described my trailer not as a *"hooch"* or a U.S. Government-issued *"can"* behind T-walls and sand bags, but as the *Fall Home Fashion Review*. I wrote that walkie-talkie radios were the latest must-have accessory for those in the know, and that in the fine, powdery dust of southern Iraq, shoe polish was my new best friend.

Friends at home asked me what small presents they could send. I really had everything material that I needed. But they sent me immeasurable gifts in their thoughts, in their e-mails. In their cards. And in their prayers, regardless of my religious beliefs. Their notes, however short, brightened my day. Their cards decorated the bulletin board by my desk. And again, I was not alone. I was humbled and awestruck by the number of stuffed animals grown men had on their office desks in Iraq, gifts and good luck charms from someone who loves them back home.

I looked routinely for reasons to laugh. I looked for comedy in the tragedy of this war. I made fun of the pink-, blue-, and white-striped *Ralph Lauren* cotton pajamas I wore faithfully to bed each night, in case I had to run for my life with no time to dress. I chuckled understandingly when the strikingly handsome security supervisor told me *it was OK* if, as one of a handful of women among nearly a thousand men, I ran to the bunker in just my flak jacket, helmet, pajamas, and boots, as long as they were not the skimpy, sexy, seductive *Victoria's Secret* kind. In a place where too many men had been away from home for far too long, *boring* had its place. Admittedly though, another scenario I vividly imagined suggested a short-lived escape fantasy of grand proportions, however fleeting it would be.

The yellow rubber duck on my desk brought a smile when I thought of *Duck and Cover*; the Boy Scout, the soldier's soldier, the Marine's Marine, my little yellow friend was already ready with his flak jacket and helmet painted right on. My colleagues complained about the weight of our flak jackets. Instead I laughed that I was just multi-tasking my doctor-ordered, weight-bearing exercise, that when I went for my next bone density scan, my physician would ask in great wide-eyed wonder what kind of super, mega-calcium drugs I had been on. I said that my helmet just gave me a good excuse for a *bad hair day*. With levity it somehow seemed easier to be brave. I built a mental catalog of images of how silly I looked lying flattened in my designer pajamas, flak jacket, and boots, with my helmet a bump on the floor, so I could laugh when I took shelter under my bed.

I grew to want a mental respite, as everyone in Iraq did, but I knew that even in my humor I must not become cavalier. Ever cognizant of the importance of day-and-night, 24/7 presence of mind, and the life or death difference it might make, I looked for distractions, but with new selectivity and care. I looked for those that would take me away while simultaneously keeping me there. And whether intentional or not, I kept one ear always tuned to the wind.

One evening when I passed through Baghdad, a *duck and cover* alarm rang out loudly at 9:30 at night. I had gone to bed early and had already fallen quickly asleep. But in an automated *Pavlovian* reflex at the first loud boom, I dove into my flak jacket and helmet, and pulled the mattress over my body as I plastered myself onto the cold, hard floor with not even a thin bed sheet underneath. Too tired that night from the accumulation of weeks of unmitigated fatigue, I fell asleep even as I lay between hard slabs and molded forms of steel, under the oppressive weight of the cotton-filled mattress that measured several inches thick. When I awoke later during the night, pressed paper-flat, I did not know how much time had passed. I had no idea if we had been given an *all-clear*. I did not know if the earlier moment's imminent threat was gone. I fell back to sleep and when I awoke again, the first thin ribbons of sunlight slipped under my mattress to herald a new day. It was the early moments of dawn. Still under the mattress in my pajamas and Personal Protective Gear on the cold, bare, linoleum-covered floor, I had survived the deadly game of Iraqi *Cat and Mouse* once more.

In those five months in Iraq I learned to live with uncertainty and fear. The unpredictability which used to be the bane of my once very orderly life became both my foe and my friend. I showed up for meetings off-site unpredictably early or late, and I sometimes cut those meetings short. I was glad when the helicopter's flight path was erratic, even as I pondered why the speed and style were so much faster and more variable than the time before. I took the routine out of my routine. I respected the life-saving value for myself and others, of surprise.

I cherished unapologetically the few times I shared embarrassingly uproarious laughs with colleagues over a simple cafeteria meal, or when the security officers made me blush. I held tight to my heart the late-night send-offs by my colleagues as I left Baghdad's *IZ* for the travel to my site. I cherished the few unguarded conversations I could have with friends or colleagues who were also in Iraq. Only with them could I talk candidly while there; only with them could I recount my experiences, share my concerns, give voice to my worries without having to self-censor and edit. Those moments were dear, and they were rare. Mostly I kept my innermost thoughts guardedly to myself.

If never fully before, in Iraq I came to realize the power of a simple smile to change someone's day. I saw with clarity the importance of asking another person if he or she were *OK*. Like a wilting flower given a much-needed drink of water, I saw a young soldier's face light up when I simply asked, *"Is everything all right?"* I saw how just giving a colleague a cold *Sprite* or a *Diet Coke* from my office refrigerator could make a little more tenable her otherwise trying afternoon. In one particularly heavy moment I was comforted by the warmth and caring of a young soldier's unsolicited hug. I have new respect for the power of a simple random act of kindness to bring some much-needed lightness to an otherwise dark or very frustrating day.

I learned to value ever more greatly my family and my friends. I tell them I love them, like I never told them before. I appreciate beyond compare those who risked their own lives to keep me safe, above all, the security guards, the soldiers, my *PSD*. *They* are *my* unsung heroes in this war. My colleagues, my co-workers, the dining room staff, and the security guards gave me a priceless gift in their smiles. I owed it to them to give them mine. Though I told him so, *Sunshine*, in his Civil Affairs uniform, with his quick stride and infinitely long legs, will never really know how much the broad smile he flashed so readily brightened my every day. His family can be proud.

I looked in awe at the men who comprised my *PSD*. Consummate professionals, those men of impeccable training, untold experience, and nerves of steel put my life ahead of their own each time we went out into town. In a most-finely choreographed dance, they positioned themselves at all times between me and the greatest perceived risk. They stood ready to take the bullets or the brunt of the car bomb or the *IED* so that I could hopefully return home safely at the end of the day. I will never be able to say *thank you* enough. I hope at least that they were exceptionally well-paid.

As I looked at the men and women of the military, some as young as seventeen, I saw a life I, myself, could not have chosen to lead. I also saw a life some of them did not really think they would face, caught up in the fervor of a zealous recruiter who maybe did not quite tell it all. But I saw a profound sense of commitment, duty, and honor. And I knew that risky as their job would otherwise be, they bore an even greater danger brought by the presence of civilians like me. I knew my mere presence put them more in harm's way. I knew each time I boarded their helicopters or their planes I was not an asset but a liability. Not a blessing, I was a minus not a plus. I hope in some small measure they can forgive me for I did not wish them any harm.

I owe an infinite and untold sum to the men and women who drove the convoys that snaked along some of the most dangerous roads in the world, just to bring some of my supplies. I do not know how many drivers and guards have been killed, but I do know the number is too high. My heart sank deep when someone told me how many convoys got hit on the road. I don't know how those men and women got in their trucks and drove.

And among a sea of American and Iraqi faces were the handsome, tanned, and serious security officers who became some of my best friends in this war. I treasured as worth more than gold the assurances by these newfound friends that they would protect me. They told me with heartfelt words that I could sleep without worry; they would watch over me from the guard stations and the gates and keep me safe. I told them I slept much better knowing they were there. Though no match for the mortars, I had not even a sliver of doubt that they would do everything they could to uphold their promises to me, to stay true to their word. It was with infinite admiration and respect that I looked at each of them every day. I cherished my conversations with those gentlemen and women who put their lives on the line every night and every day to protect mine. They brought me laughter with mealtime jokes about scrambled eggs and *Texas Pete's Hot Sauce*. I relished their tales of wild animals, of beautiful colonial cities, and relaxing beaches back home. Reassured by their courage, their promises, their faith, their stories, and their unassuming warmth, they took me away, if only momentarily, to a place where things did not go *boom* in the night.

In those months of trying to make a difference in Iraq, if and where I could, I frequently questioned why I was there. But I reminded myself of the little boy who, on finding many starfish stranded on the beach, threw one back into the sea. When asked what difference it made when there were so many starfish lying about, he said it made a big difference to *that* one, pointing to the one he threw back.

In my time in Iraq I had endless nights and eternal days of hoping to cheat the insurgents of their murderous goal. Of dodging mortars and bullets and *IEDs* and *EFPs*. Of standing tall and lying low. Of knowing that hard as I might think I had it, others had it much worse.

I hope for everyone that this war will end soon. And I hope that one day in the future I will be able to feel serenity again in tranquil days. *That I will be able to remember what peace there may be in silence,* as Max Ehrmann said. And as I rest in the luxury and quiet of my own home once again, I hope that I do not forget the hard-learned lessons of my time in Iraq, so that my vigilant days and my sleepless nights will not have been in vain.

Godspeed

Godspeed

I *can sit with the old men now.* It was a long time coming, and the roads I traveled have been filled with adventure, danger, friendship, laughter, happiness, and tears. Through the experiences I have had, and the lessons I have learned, I have at last earned the honor to be able to join the wise old men.

But the story must not end there. Someday I will tell Jakub, and Katherine, Duncan, Yacob, Celia, Will, and Ben my ventures. They are tales best told in a quiet voice in the soft light of a kerosene lamp. I will tell them about places with names like *Mandalay, Budapest, Samarqand, Baghdad, Djibouti, Phnom Penh,* and *Katmandu.* I will recount tales of vast deserts, dense jungles, and mountains so high they touch the heavens. I will talk of men with piercing eyes and of women whose beauty makes others melt.

I will tell about cobras and gorillas and gazelle. About lustrous silks, fragrant spices, and shining gold. About bush planes and ferries, rubber dinghies, camel caravans, and mule carts. I will talk of lovers, and lepers, and curries, and tea. I hope after each story they will ask for more. And I hope one day they will travel the world as well.

Godspeed. Have a rich and wondrous journey. Somewhere, the old men are waiting for you, too.